DATE DUE

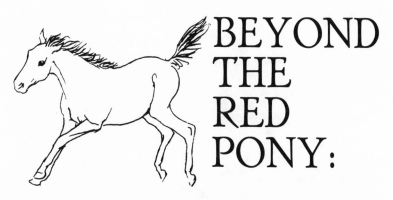

BEYOND THE RED PONY:

A Reader's Companion to Steinbeck's Complete Short Stories

by
R. S. Hughes

The Scarecrow Press, Inc.
Metuchen, N.J., & London • 1987

Library of Congress Cataloging-in-Publication Data

Hughes, R. S., 1948–
    Beyond the red pony.

    Bibliography: p.
    Includes index.
    1. Steinbeck, John, 1902–1968   —Plots.
2. Steinbeck, John, 1902–1968–   —Criticism
and interpretation. I. Title.
PS3537.T3234Z7146 1987   813'.52   86–31567
ISBN 0–8108–1970–8

For KIFF HUGHES
and
BOB HUGHES,

my good parents

CONTENTS

CHAPTER THREE

CHAPTER FOUR

PREFACE

Beyond The Red Pony is intended as a practical handbook for teachers, students, and general readers who wish to discover the full breadth and variety of John Steinbeck's short fiction. My aims in the book are two: 1) to provide the first comprehensive study of Steinbeck's short fiction including every story he wrote--published and unpublished; and 2) to establish an up-to-date and complete bibliography of these stories. No one before has attempted to discuss all of these tales in a single forum, especially the little-known pieces which comprise more than half of Steinbeck's work in the short story genre.

Several people have generously assisted me during the writing of Beyond The Red Pony. J. Albert Robbins, Professor Emeritus, Indiana University, carefully guided me through the early stages of the project; Carlton A. "Dook" Sheffield graciously shared with me his insights and recollections about his life-long friend, John Steinbeck; A. Grove Day, Professor Emeritus, University of Hawaii at Manoa, through his delightful reminiscences about Steinbeck, also provided me with new perspectives; and Tetsumaro Hayashi, Professor of English, Ball State University, and Editor of the Steinbeck Quarterly, encouraged and inspired me with his many kindnesses. Sue Cowing, LaRene Despain, Felix Smith, and Debra Weiner offered useful editorial tips during our Honolulu writing-group meetings. And, finally, my special thanks to Charlene Avallone whose perceptiveness as a reader has been, as always, invaluable to me.

Financial and logistical support for Beyond The Red Pony has come in the form of a research grant from Indiana University, a course reduction, travel grant, and research leave from the University of Hawaii at Manoa, and typing services provided by the Decio Faculty Steno Pool at the

University of Notre Dame: Cheryl Reed, Forestine Blake, Margaret Jasiewicz, Nancy Kegler, Nila Gerhold, and Shirley Vogel--thank you all for your assistance. Arts and Letters Associate Dean Roger B. Skurski also kindly provided me with a private office at the University of Notre Dame. Reid and Karen Woodward, Tom and Buzzy Stokes, John and Judy Michener, Kiff Hughes, and Bob Hughes--my California family--helped me immeasurably by paying for the typing of a complete early version of Beyond The Red Pony and by making possible my numerous visits to Steinbeck Country.

Portions of this book have been previously published in different form and are reprinted with the permission of the Steinbeck Quarterly and Harvard Library Bulletin. The frontispiece and several additional photographs are reproduced with the permission of the Salinas Valley Guild and the John Steinbeck Library, Salinas, California. Special thanks to Maurice Dunbar for permission to use his photo of "The Castle" in the Corral de Tierra and to Karen Woodward and Sabrina Chavers of Carmel Valley for their artwork.

Chapter One

INTRODUCTION AND STORIES
FROM THE 1920s

When John Steinbeck won the Nobel Prize for literature in
1962, Arthur Mizener used the occasion to reflect on the new
laureate's career. Although in his New York Times Book Review essay Mizener finds numerous flaws in Steinbeck's novels, he gives almost unqualified praise to the four stories
which comprise The Red Pony (1945). Mizener credits this
work with "an integrity, a responsibility to experience and a
consequent unity of surface and symbol" that Steinbeck never
duplicated.[1]

The Red Pony has long been a favorite with readers
too. We share Jody Tiflin's delight upon receiving his red
pony, and his anguish at its death. We understand his awe
of Gitano, the mysterious Indian who returns to the Tiflin
ranch to die; and we praise Jody's compassion for his grandfather, the aging wagon train leader rendered useless by time.
Near the shadows of the brooding "Great Mountains," the
Tiflin family resides in a distinctively "Western" landscape,
yet Jody's initiation into the secrets of life and death touches
us regardless of our backgrounds or origins. For good reason, then, The Red Pony volume contains Steinbeck's best-
known stories.

Even though these four tales have remained popular
through the years, many readers have yet to discover Steinbeck's short fiction beyond The Red Pony. Steinbeck wrote
nearly fifty stories: nine in The Pastures of Heaven (1932),
fifteen in The Long Valley (1938), and a dozen more scat-
tered in back issues of Collier's, Harper's, Reader's Digest,
Punch, and the Atlantic. Six additional stories remain in
manuscript and numerous others appear among his war and

1

travel dispatches. Since half of Steinbeck's tales were never
collected, few readers have experienced such biographically
important works as "His Father" (1948), "The Summer Before" (1955), and "Case of the Hotel Ghost" (1957). Even
Steinbeck's O. Henry Memorial Award-winning "Affair at 7,
Rue de M---" (1955), and his refreshingly terse, "How Mr.
Hogan Robbed a Bank" (1956) have not reached the large
audience they deserve.

These little known, yet important, stories are neglected
by critics, as well as readers. Book-length surveys of American short fiction generally discuss The Long Valley, but not
Steinbeck's work of the preceding or later decades. In The
Short Story in America: 1900-1950 (1952), Ray B. West lim-
its his analysis to Steinbeck's tales of the 30s. In The American Short Story (1973), Arthur Voss also examines these
stories exclusively.[2] And in the more recent Critical Survey
of Short Fiction (1981), James K. Folsom appraises just two
Steinbeck works, both from his 1938 collection.[3] Even veteran Steinbeck scholars Peter Lisca and Warren French have
not considered the author's entire canon of short fiction.[4]

Beyond The Red Pony provides the first comprehensive
study of Steinbeck's short stories. Every known Steinbeck
story is appraised--his popular work of the 1930s, as well as
his forgotten tales of earlier and later decades. Since Steinbeck's short fiction spans more than three decades--from 1924
to 1957--his development as a story writer will be approached
in three phases. The first phase, the 1920s, comprises his
period of apprenticeship; the second, the 1930s, his rise to
artistic maturity and international fame; and the third, the
1940s and 50s, his turning inward and experimenting with
new forms and styles.

Apprenticeship in the 1920s

Although he had been composing stories in his attic
bedroom while attending Salinas High School, Steinbeck's
apprenticeship as a story writer actually began during his
student days at Stanford University. Robert DeMott explains
that Steinbeck "enrolled in eleven English courses" at Stanford, including journalism, news and essay writing, composition, and in 1924, "Edith Mirrielees' English 136, Short Story
Writing, which he later remembered as one of the best

[courses] he ever took."[5] Steinbeck's gratitude to his
favorite Stanford teacher is evidenced in the preface he
wrote some forty years later to Mirrielees' revised text,
Story Writing (1962).[6] When Steinbeck was her student,
Mirrielees read the young author's "Fingers of Cloud" (1924)
and encouraged him to expand his technical horizons by experimenting with characters and situations beyond his own
experience. Apparently following her suggestion, Steinbeck
dabbled in fantasy emulating James Branch Cabell, Donn
Byrne, and other popular writers with whom he was acquainted. Consequently his subsequent stories, "Adventures in Arcademy" (1924), "The Gifts of Iban" (1927), and
several unpublished tales reveal "a pronounced subservience
to popular literary models,"[7] as DeMott points out. Though
Steinbeck's characters are sometimes wooden and lack reason-
able motivation, he showed promise in the richness of his descriptions and his brilliant imagery--fanciful settings where
nymphs and fauns dance in a world of colorful make-believe.
Such joyous scenes do not abrogate, however, Cabellian
themes of loneliness, disillusionment, and rejection.

Coming of Age in the 1930s

Steinbeck reached maturity as a story writer and as a
novelist in his second phase during the 1930s. His first volume containing short fiction, The Pastures of Heaven (1932),
invites comparison with Sherwood Anderson's Winesburg, Ohio
(1919). Like Anderson, Steinbeck probes the psychological
complexities of seemingly simple characters who often prove
to be extraordinary. In Pastures, Steinbeck makes several
technical advances: his characters, including his first memorable women, seem rounder and more believable; his plotting
becomes more unified through carefully drawn symbols; and
his settings, as he turns to the California region he knows
best, become more realistic.

In The Long Valley (1938), which includes The Red Pony,
Steinbeck deals indirectly with social, economic, and political
issues of the day.[8] Yet although some critics have argued
to the contrary, these stories show Steinbeck to be more an
artist than a social reformer.[9] In "The White Quail" (1935)
and "The Chrysanthemums" (1937), Steinbeck echoes the sensitive, lyrical style of Fitzgerald.[10] In "Flight" (1938), he
develops a terse and laconic idiom, reminiscent of Hemingway.

And in "Johnny Bear" (1937), Steinbeck turns away from action, and focuses--as does Anderson--on the pathetic and
grotesque. Ostensibly linking these stories of various styles
and themes is the "long" Salinas Valley, a ninety-mile stretch
of rich farm land which Steinbeck evokes with the vividness
of Faulkner's "Yoknapatawpha County."

New Directions in the 1940s and 1950s

Steinbeck's uncollected stories of his final phase differ
from his Long Valley tales in several ways: while nearly
every story of the 1930s takes place in "Steinbeck Country,"
settings in the later pieces include an Indian village in Mexico, a famous hotel in London, and a distinguished home near
the Champs-Elysées in Paris. Backdrops are more often urban than pastoral, and those in America feature the eastern
seaboard as well as the western. When nearing the end of
his career, Steinbeck becomes increasingly autobiographical. He breaks his own precedent by modeling characters after himself and members of his immediate family.

Besides providing rare glimpses into Steinbeck's personal life, these later tales show remarkable diversity in
style: loose and episodic ("The Summer Before" [1955]),
tight, spare, and objective ("How Mr. Hogan Robbed a Bank"
[1956]), allegorical ("The Short-Short Story of Mankind"
[1955]), as well as the elevated, Poesque style of "Affair at
7, Rue de M---" (1955). Steinbeck also experiments with
several new themes including divorce, nuclear holocaust, and
a child's discovery of sexual differences. Thus, several
tales of the 1940s and 50s speak directly to the times, two of
them winning the O. Henry Memorial Award. Steinbeck produced these stories near the end of his career, more than
thirty years after his first piece of short fiction appeared.
Yet "Fingers of Cloud" (1924), as we shall now see,
foreshadows the characters and settings of Steinbeck's most
popular writing.

"Fingers of Cloud:
A Satire on College Protervity"
(1924)

In January 1921, Steinbeck took a job as a straw boss

at the Spreckles sugar-beet ranch near Chualar, California. In charge of a half dozen laborers who loaded "railroad cars with great burlap bags of beets," Steinbeck shared a bunkhouse with these ranch hands and ate in their common mess. The aspiring author's co-workers proved to be "coarse, uneducated, hard-drinking roustabouts" who came from Mexico, China, Portugal, and probably the Philippines.[11]

That Steinbeck had in mind his experiences with these co-workers at the Spreckles ranch when he wrote "Fingers of Cloud" is suggested by the story: Gertie, a teenage orphan and runaway, climbs a hill to gaze upon the drifting clouds. When a huge gray cloud brushes her eyelids closed, she sleeps until awakened by a downpour. Gertie rushes to find shelter in a nearby bunkhouse where Filipino ranchhands are playing cards and bickering with a red-faced bootlegger. Pedro, the crew boss, hurries Gertie into his bedroom and emerges later announcing his intention to marry her. For a time the couple are happy, until Pedro begins beating Gertie after his hot days working in the beet fields. Repulsed by Pedro's dark, sweaty back and the decaying horse heads he keeps in a fire barrel, Gertie leaves him and returns to the hill where she began, once again to admire the fingers of cloud.

Even though the story's subtitle, "A Satire on College Protervity," suggests student life as its subject, Steinbeck never mentions his days on the Stanford campus in "Fingers of Cloud." As Nelson Valjean points out, only the wisps of clouds in the story may have emanated from the young author's observations while at college. The fields, bunkhouse, and foreign laborers, on the other hand, almost certainly grew out of his employment at the Spreckles ranch.[12]

Published in the Stanford Spectator, February, 1924, "Fingers of Cloud" has received scant attention in critical studies, with most mentions consisting of a one or two-sentence paraphrase. Peter Lisca calls the story "an account of a subnormal girl who marries a migrant Filipino laborer."[13] Joseph Fontenrose refers in passing to Pedro and Gertie as "imbeciles."[14] Thomas Kiernan simply labels them "weird."[15] Although critics generally see the story as an apprentice piece bearing little relation to Steinbeck's later works, Valjean has shown that in its bunkhouse setting, "Fingers of Cloud" foreshadows Of Mice and Men (1937).[16] Notice the similar furnishings in the two bunkhouses:

"Fingers of Cloud":

> Burlap tacked loosely on the walls, a littered
> floor of dust colored wood, a few boxes to sit on,
> and the fat-bellied stove--that was the lounging
> room of the bunkhouse. Three pock-marked brown
> men played cards on the floor under a coal oil
> lamp.[17]

Of Mice and Men:

> The bunkhouse was a long, rectangular building
> ... the floor unpainted.... Near one wall there was
> a black cast-iron stove.... In the middle of the
> room stood a big square table littered with playing
> cards, and around it were grouped boxes for the
> players to sit on.[18]

In addition to its likeness in setting to Of Mice and
Men, "Fingers of Cloud" provides crude prototypes for characters in Steinbeck's later fiction. Pedro and his whiskey-
drinking workers resemble Danny and his Paisano friends in
Tortilla Flat (1935), and the seductive Gertie suggests Cur-
ley's wife in Of Mice and Men. Even such an incidental character as the bootlegger, a "large red man" who is eventually
duped by the ranch hands, resembles Torrelli, the sometimes
unwitting supplier of wine in Tortilla Flat, and Mr. Edwards,
the hefty, deceived whoremaster in East of Eden (1952).

Although Pedro, Gertie, and the bootlegger are pre-
cursors of later Steinbeck characters, only Gertie is fully
sketched in the story. She appears as an animal with white
hair resembling sheep's wool, the pliant muscles of a dog,
and high-pitched scream of a coyote. Gertie talks in a lazy
slang, sprinkling her speech with "ain't" (p. 108), while
Pedro utters impeccable English ("'I say that I am going to
marry the woman'" [p. 106] on some occasions, and pidgin
("'I think I buy blue dress for you. You like?'" [p. 108])
on others. Pedro's inconsistent speech suggests that Steinbeck, in the first phase of his career, was just beginning to
develop what would later become his masterful ear for dialogue.

Though obviously an apprentice story, "Fingers of
Cloud" shows Steinbeck's strengths as a young writer. While
struggling with plotting and character motivation, he suc-
ceeded in creating the crisply-drawn bunkhouse setting he
would immortalize a decade later in Of Mice and Men.

"Adventures in Arcademy:
A Journey into the Ridiculous"
(1924)

"Adventures in Arcademy," Steinbeck's second published story, differs from his first in several ways: the
plot, involving a brief allegorical journey, is complicated by
obscure allusions. The characters include several talking
squirrels, buffalos, penguins, and a gray goose. The Stanford University setting is stylized into a surreal dream where
"trees bear striped candies" and "purple pomegranates."[19]
The point of view becomes first-person, rather than Steinbeck's earlier third person stance. The narrator's language
seems deliberately evasive, veiling his ridicule of Stanford
students, faculty, and administrators. As a result, "Adventures in Arcademy" is a satirical allegory "with meanings
sometimes hidden almost too well."[20]

The story, even in its bare outline, seems bizarre:
The narrator strolls along a white shell road, when an old
man wearing pants of colorful glass explains that the narrator too may someday acquire some. Other people join them
walking along the white shell road, which eventually changes
color to light pink. They reach a ticket booth, where the
surroundings change hue to red (Stanford's school color).
Several frenzied animals chase onlookers, as technicians labor over test tubes and proclaim, "'Gasoline and alcohol will
not mix!'" Nearby, women play in "thick, black mud" around
a pool, while a gray goose cautions them not to get wet.
Soon the narrator is separated from other sojourners by a
pouter pigeon, who calls him a heretic. Then several penguins denounce him for being only partly red. Suddenly he
is ousted from the shell road; walls close behind him and he
sits outside entirely alone.

Carlton "Dook" Sheffield, a college roommate and life-
long friend of Steinbeck, believes that even if all identifiable
allusions in "Adventures in Arcademy" were explained, parts
of the story would still remain a mystery. He contends that
Steinbeck may have engaged in deliberate "obfuscation," so
that even his classmates would not have been able to recognize some of the more obscure references. Sheffield conjec-
tures that the "shell road" in the story is "the path to and
through Stanford and education." The technicians' exclama-
tion, "'Gasoline and alcohol will not mix,'" Sheffield identifies
as "a favorite admonition by [Stanford] President Ray Lyman

Wilbur in a campaign against student drinking." Since Steinbeck wrote the story during Prohibition, President Wilbur no
doubt intended his words to protect Stanford from legal em-
barrassment, as well as to preserve the morals of its students.
Sheffield further suggests that the "gray goose," who cautions
mud-besmirched coeds to avoid the pool, mimics Dean of Women
Mary Yost, who frequently lectured Stanford women on purity,
"especially of a sexual nature." Among the story's other
creatures, the penguins who rush the narrator off the shell
road may represent the Stanford faculty, with whom Steinbeck
had frequent "brushes" when he neglected to attend classes
and take exams.[21]

     The obscurity of these allusions reflects some of Stein-
beck's most important influences during his college years,
Stanford English professor, Edith Mirrielees and novelist,
James Branch Cabell. When Steinbeck enrolled in Mirrielees'
story writing course, he had already completed "Fingers of
Cloud." Mirrielees gave new direction to Steinbeck's work
by suggesting he invent his next story (very likely "Adventures") totally out of his imagination.[22] The trees bearing
"striped candies" and "purple pomegranates" and the several
bizarre animals in the story resulted perhaps from Mirrielees'
advice. In addition, Steinbeck's surreal setting echoes the
fanciful backdrops of James Branch Cabell's popular novel,
Jurgen (1922).[23] Steinbeck also employs typical Cabellian
themes: rejection, loneliness, and the shattering of masculine dreams.

     In sum, "Adventures in Arcademy" includes a cast of
strange characters and an eerie, other-worldly locale. Steinbeck lets his young fancy run wild. Yet in this playful and
obscure tale, we cannot miss the narrator's feeling of alienation, perhaps reflecting Steinbeck's growing unhappiness with
college by 1924. The unnamed protagonist communicates with
none of his fellow travelers and receives little encouragement
from university officials. The story serves as allegorical
memoir of the young writer's intermittent journey along the
road to a university degree. Like the narrator in "Adventures," Steinbeck left Stanford without graduating, little
more than one year after this odd allegory appeared.

UNPUBLISHED STORIES
(1924-26)

Introduction

        June 1925 marked the end of Steinbeck's college career.
Through the influence of his Stanford classmate, Toby Street,
he signed on as a maintenance man and mail driver at Fallen
Leaf Lake resort in the Sierras, near Lake Tahoe. Steinbeck
worked there with Street for several months into the autumn
until cold weather forced them back to civilization--Street to
Stanford, and Steinbeck to visit Dook Sheffield who was
teaching at Occidental College in Los Angeles. But soon
Steinbeck was to leave California and begin his long and
ambivalent association with New York City.[24] In late November, 1925, he boarded the rusting vessel, Katrina,
bound for Manhattan via the Panama Canal and Cuba. Using the hundred dollars which he had intended to settle on
in New York, Steinbeck escorted an attractive woman around
Havana and indulged in "broad rum drinks like tubs of soaking fruit."[25] On account of this and other romantic inter-
ludes during his voyage, he disembarked in New York with
only three dollars in his pocket. Through necessity, Steinbeck took a job wheeling 150-pound barrows of cement on
the construction site of Madison Square Garden. The pay
was good, but the heavy labor left him little energy to write.
Eventually he quit and with the help of an influential uncle
became a cadet newspaper reporter for the New York American.

        Steinbeck had not sailed to Manhattan merely to work
odd jobs. He had come with a purpose: to establish himself as a writer in the literary capital of the United States.[26]
Nonetheless, his stay lasted a brief six months, hardly time
enough for an unknown author of twenty-three to break into
New York's publishing world. Since Steinbeck's attempts to
advance his career were at first limited to his spare time after long hours as a day laborer and later as an errant reporter, it is not surprising that he failed to achieve his goal.
Once he realized that New York had got the better of him,
he needed no urging to leave; he accepted a working berth
on a ship bound for California. In his own words: "The
city had beaten the pants off me. Whatever it required to
get ahead, I didn't have."[27] Although he was encouraged
by one editor of a book publishing firm, Steinbeck sailed

away from New York in June, 1926 with no better prospects
than when he had arrived six months earlier.

Accounts vary as to the exact number of stories Steinbeck wrote during this period. Thomas Kiernan says Steinbeck offered a total of nine tales to McBride & Co., book
publishers.[28] Nelson Valjean is less specific, saying that
Steinbeck sent a "batch of his stories" to McBride and then,
upon the request of editor Guy Holt, wrote "a half-dozen
more."[29] Dook Sheffield estimates that the young author
wrote up to twelve.[30] Amasa "Ted" Miller, who befriended
Steinbeck at Stanford and later saw him "several times a
week" during his 1926-27 stay in Manhattan, says he "wrote
many stories in New York, perhaps more than a dozen."[31]
And Jackson J. Benson believes Steinbeck may have added
to the total by revising several earlier tales to conform to
the Manhattan theme of his projected volume for McBride.[32]

Regardless of the precise number, some or all of these
stories were rejected by a new editor at McBride, who had
replaced Guy Holt. Steinbeck stormed (or was thrown) out
of the office with the unwanted manuscripts in hand. Very
likely several of the texts have not survived. Steinbeck was
capable of destroying his own creations, as Dook Sheffield
once sadly learned. In Pacific Grove one afternoon, Sheffield
watched his unpredictable friend toss ten years' correspondence between the two men into a fire, simply because it contained samples of what Steinbeck called his "bad writing."[33]
Just as he burned his letters to Sheffield, so too may Steinbeck have burned or scuttled some of these early stories.
One which probably met this fate is recalled by Amasa Miller:

> It was about a woman and a cockroach.... The
> woman was disenchanted with her wishy-washy hus-
> band or boyfriend, and the story was a sort of al-
> legory of the development of her feelings about him,
> played out by relating her attitude toward the in-
> sect. It [the cockroach] was attempting to get
> around some obstacle and kept falling over on its
> back. Several times she gently righted it, but when
> its failures persisted she finally stepped on it or hit
> it with something, and so killed it. I have no idea
> where the draft of that or any other stories ended
> up. John may very well have destroyed them.[34]

Like the cockroach in this Steinbeck piece, reminiscent
of Kafka's "The Metamorphosis" (1913), the manuscript itself
does not survive. Fortunately, several other texts have.
Six unpublished stories from this period are safely held in
Harvard and Stanford University libraries; Harvard's Houghton Library owns four: "East Third Street," "The Days of
Long Marsh," "The Nail," and "The Nymph and Isobel"; and
Stanford's Department of Special Collections holds the other
two: "The White Sister of Fourteenth Street" and an untitled
Christmas story. Benson believes that some of these tales
are of "publishable quality" and seem "far more advanced
than anything written by Hemingway, Faulkner, or Fitzgerald at the same age."[35]

Since these Steinbeck manuscripts are available for inspection, it may be justifiably asked why they have remained
so long in obscurity. Six largely unknown stories by a major
American author would ordinarily become the focal point of
critical activity. One reason these early Steinbeck stories
have attracted so little attention is that for many years the
texts were in the hands of private collectors. A second
reason involves a 1972 Steinbeck Quarterly article question-
ing the authenticity of the four stories owned by the Houghton Library. In "Four Dubious Steinbeck Stories," Clifford
L. Lewis calls the tales bogus: "Steinbeck scholars should
be informed that the four short stories held in the Steinbeck
Collection at Harvard's Houghton Library were not written
by John Steinbeck."[36] To understand why this statement is
incorrect, we must step back in time to 1926 when Steinbeck's
first sojourn in New York came to an end.

Upon sailing home in June, 1926, Steinbeck either
carried his surviving story manuscripts with him to San
Francisco or left them with someone in Manhattan. Amasa
Miller would have been a likely recipient, since he had been
promoting Steinbeck's work there and was eventually to sell
to McBride & Co. the first Steinbeck novel, Cup of Gold
(1929). But although he knew about the stories Steinbeck
wrote in New York, Miller says that none of them was con-
signed to him.[37] Whether the stories voyaged west with
Steinbeck in 1926 or remained for a time in New York, four
surfaced nearly a decade later in California.

During early 1935, Steinbeck wrote to Los Angeles

Times book critic Wilbur Needham that he wished to discuss
plans for a forthcoming novel.[38] Perhaps Steinbeck chose
Needham as a literary consultant because the Times critic
had written several friendly reviews of Steinbeck's work,
particularly Pastures of Heaven (1932) and To a God Unknown (1933).[39] Steinbeck probably met with Needham
sometime in the mid-1930s and then, or soon thereafter, gave
him the four unpublished stories. Needham, in turn, gave
these four texts to literary historian and librarian, Lawrence
Clark Powell. That Needham received the four stories from
Steinbeck is almost a certainty, says Powell, who became
acquainted with Needham in the mid-1930s:

> I was working in [Jake] Zeitlin's Bookshop,
> 1934-36, and Needham (who later became a book-
> seller) was in and out of the shop. When Needham
> learned of my early interest in Steinbeck ... he
> gave me the Steinbeck typescripts.... I see no
> reason to believe that the stories were not written
> by Steinbeck. He is the last one in the world to
> pass off another's work as his own--and I am quite
> sure that Needham received them directly from
> Steinbeck.[40]

In 1941 Powell sold the four typescripts to the Houghton Library, where they remain today.[41]

    One thing that distinguishes most of the six Steinbeck
stories owned by the Houghton and Stanford University Libraries is their New York City settings. Except for "The
Days of Long Marsh" and "The Nail" (discussed below),
these early pieces take place specifically in Lower Manhattan.
While a reporter for the American, Steinbeck's regular beat
was the federal courts in their old Park Row offices, just
minutes away from the Lower East Side, Chinatown, and
Little Italy.[42] He eventually became familiar with this district and accumulated enough material about its people and
environs for several short stories, four having survived.[43]
"East Third Street" takes place among the boarding houses
and late-night diners of the Lower East Side. Steinbeck's
untitled Christmas story depicts the brutal contrast between
Manhattan's sparkling commercial towers and its dingy,
cockroach-infested boarding houses. "The White Sister of
Fourteenth Street" is set in the old Fourteenth Street Theatre (105 W. 14th Street) and features a protagonist, Angelo,

with roots in Little Italy. And "The Nymph and Isobel" has
as its backdrop a small park probably near Chinatown, where
Isobel's unwanted escort promises her supper.

Steinbeck's four Lower Manhattan stories, sharing the
same 1920s period with Fitzgerald's The Great Gatsby (1925),
picture a much different New York from that of Gatsby and
his occasional friends. To them Manhattan is the bright and
dazzling playground of Fifth Avenue between Fiftieth Street
and Central Park, whose focal point is the fashionable Plaza
Hotel. Steinbeck's fictional terrain is farther south and closer to the East River. And while Fitzgerald's protagonists
are generally affluent, Steinbeck's stagnate as warehousemen,
garage attendants, and garment industry workers. They re-
side in America's melting pot: tenement and boarding houses
on the Lower East Side. Stark buildings, sickly trees, and
narrow streets form the backdrop of their lives. Beneath
the shadows of an oppressive, ragged skyline, races inter-
mingle and cross, much as they had done three decades earlier under the gaze of another promising young writer, Stephen
Crane.

Although Steinbeck's Lower Manhattan Stories take
place during the prohibition and boom years of the twenties,
they share characteristics with the sub-genre that in the
1890s Crane advanced to a fine art: Bowery fiction, or literature of the slums. The hallmark of Bowery fiction is
graphic descriptions of "foulness, dampness, noise, crowding," and squalor, thus revealing the slums to be a "breed-
er of physical and moral weakness," especially prostitution.[44]
Steinbeck's stories differ from Crane's in that the latter's
focus on the air of hopelessness that surrounds the Bowery.
We need only compare Crane's "An Experiment in Misery"
(1894) with Steinbeck's "East Third Street" (1924-26) to notice this difference. Both stories feature downtrodden male
slum-dwellers; yet while Crane's protagonist, without home
or job, withers beneath New York's towering skyline, Steinbeck's counterpart rises to a moral victory of sorts. Steinbeck's Bowery stories give us at least faint promise of a
better life.

While Crane seldom mentions the ethnic heritage of his
slum-dwellers, Steinbeck often does. New York City as
"melting pot" looms large in Steinbeck's work; one of his
protagonists, Angelo or "Wappapa," in "The White Sister,"

is Italian. The ethnic backgrounds of some other characters
can be determined by their names, such as Moe Greenberg,
the Jewish shopkeeper who employs the heroine in "The
Nymph and Isobel." Considering this ethnic diversity among
characters, we would expect to find linguistic differences as
well. However, while Steinbeck attempts to render dialectal
peculiarities--as we saw in "Fingers of Cloud"--he had not
yet developed the accurate ear which enabled him to capture
realistic conversation in The Grapes of Wrath (1939).

Since Steinbeck did not date his unpublished stories of
the 1920s, the four extant texts set in Lower Manhattan will
be considered according to their seasonal backdrops. "East
Third Street" takes place in November, the month in late
1925 when Steinbeck would have arrived in New York City.
Steinbeck's untitled Christmas story comes next, its December setting evidenced by winter snows which the lonely protagonist fears he may not survive. The action in "The White
Sister of Fourteenth Street" takes place several months later
in spring, and that of "The Nymph and Isobel" on a sultry
evening in the beginning of summer. Since Steinbeck returned to California in late June, 1926, this would have been
the last season he saw during his first sojourn in Manhattan.
His two remaining unpublished texts from this period, "The
Days of Long Marsh" (set in California) and "The Nail" (set
in biblical Canaan), will be examined after the Lower Manhattan stories.

"East Third Street"
(ca. 1924-26)

Cowardice is the theme of the first Lower Manhattan
story, "East Third Street."[45] Steinbeck focuses on this
perennial trait of human character by recounting one fright-
ful evening in the life of a small, self-conscious working man
named Vinch. Even his distorted memories remind Vinch he
has always been a coward. During childhood, he ran trem-
bling from thick-legged little boys; in adolescence, he slunk
away from ruffians on the streets of New York; and as an
adult, he passively endures drubbings at the hands of his
drinking chums. It is fitting, then, that Vinch equates his
own name with cowardice. Yet his conduct one night in a
secluded barroom on East Third Street suggests that Vinch
is a braver man than either he or the reader imagine.

The story unfolds on a chilly November evening with
Vinch pacing nervously along East Third Street. Craving a
whiskey before bed, he walks to Frank's Place but lacks the
courage to enter. When three other thirsty men happen
along, Vinch anxiously follows them through a long dark
hallway until he trips and falls into the drinking room.
Laughter explodes as a crowd of drunken men muss Vinch's
hair and clothing. Yet he quietly conceals his anger. When
Frank brings around a tray of drinks, Vinch takes one and
disappears into a corner. Suddenly from the hallway a huge
Sicilian, Dominick, lumbers in. Everyone freezes. By this
time, Vinch is becoming intoxicated and begins to remember
his disagreeable past. Hatred for his father, in particular,
wells inside him. Just when Vinch can no longer contain his
anger, Dominick approaches him for money. Without thinking, Vinch smashes the huge Sicilian in the jaw, and he falls
to the floor. Then the enraged Vinch flies at the other men
in the room, until Frank and his two big sons pin his arms
and throw him back onto East Third Street. Vinch dashes to
his boarding house, safe from the rampaging Sicilian.

As he did in his college stories, Steinbeck uses animal
imagery in "East Third Street" to illustrate traits of human
character. For example, early in the story he shows how
Vinch's father cruelly wounds his bird dog for missing a
point, and in the same spirit whips his son for the most
trivial offenses. The wounded pointer becomes a symbol
for the emotionally crippled Vinch. The importance of this
symbol is underscored when Vinch once imagines himself
groveling on his stomach before Dominick like the bird dog.
"East Third Street" marks the first time in Steinbeck's fiction that a dog evokes the physical or emotional states of
human beings. "Darling," the canine mascot of the Palace
Flophouse in Cannery Row (1945), provides an apt example
of how Steinbeck later developed this motif. The long association in Steinbeck's work between man and his best
friend culminates in his October 8, 1955 Saturday Review
article "Random Thoughts on Random Dogs" and in the better known, Travels with Charley (1962), where Charley often becomes a barometer of his master's moods and feelings.

Besides the crippled pointer, Steinbeck employs other
animal images to characterize Vinch, including a horse, cat,
rabbit, and bird. But more pervasive than this animal
imagery in "East Third Street" are images of darkness,

light, and color. While Steinbeck paints a dark picture of
Manhattan low-life during the 1920s, Vinch is nearly always
moving toward some source of light. On dusky streets or
in nearly black hallways, light--either moonlight or incan-
descent light--draws Vinch onward. And, as in "Adventures in Arcademy," the color red pervades. The drinking
room is illuminated with one lamp covered with a red shade.
Upon the faded wallpaper and even in the smoke-filled air,
red predominates, and turns the atmosphere of the room--
men, whiskey, and smoke--into a swirling sea of crimson.
The presence of red in the story suggests the harshness
and danger of New York's boarding house districts and some
of its inhabitants.

Untitled Christmas Story
(ca. 1925-26)

While fear and loneliness are recurrent themes in his
early short pieces, none suggests Steinbeck's own desolation
so much as his untitled story of Christmas Eve in Manhattan. 46 William, the autobiographical protagonist, spends the
evening alone trying to fend off painful memories. When the
elevator operator of his building says "Merry Christmas"
while holding out his hand, William gives him a half dollar
and walks out into the gusting snow. Above the storm, he
sees the bright orange tip of the Metropolitan (life insur-
ance) tower, which he cynically calls the new star of redemption. He considers buying a Christmas tree and finding
someone on the street to share the evening with, but finally
reconciles himself to reading Cellini, who makes him feel un-
conquerable. A fur-clad woman with rouge smeared on her
face then emerges from a darkened doorway and asks, "Merry
Christmas?" Declining her proposition, William hands her a
dollar and trudges through the snow back to his room. Inside, he curls up with his volume of Cellini, but it fails to
bring him comfort. A pair of shiny boots and a talking
stuffed raccoon in the room evoke painful memories of a little
house, a windmill, and a woman singing softly. Rather than
suffer these recollections, William locks the boots in his clos-
et and kicks the raccoon until its cotton stuffing falls out.

Steinbeck probably wrote this untitled story in the
Gramercy Park section of Manhattan during Christmas, 1925.
Upon completing the manuscript, he sent a carbon to his

former Stanford flame, Margaret Gemmell. Steinbeck explains
in a 1926 letter to Gemmell that the story is unedited and
strives to communicate a feeling rather than to depict a series of actions.[47] The feeling he refers to in this letter is
no doubt loneliness, and perhaps alienation and resulting de-
fensiveness. According to Dook Sheffield Steinbeck may
have conceived of and begun the story on Christmas Eve to
ward off the agony of aloneness on this usually festive occasion.[48] Steinbeck also inverts the meaning of that warm hol-
iday impulse to give, the "Christmas spirit." Although the
soft-hearted William dispenses his money freely to the elevator operator and prostitute, his generosity contrasts with
the greed he finds in them and elsewhere on the streets of
Manhattan.

Two curious features in Steinbeck's Christmas story
include the stuffed raccoon and William's trusted volume of
Cellini. Sheffield suggests that this talking raccoon may
plague William just as Scrooge in Dickens' The Christmas
Carol (1842) is haunted by various spirits.[49] William reads
Cellini's autobiography, on the other hand, to bolster his
sagging confidence. Italian sculptor, goldsmith and author
Benvenuto Cellini (1500-1571) probably appealed to the lonely and insecure William (and to Steinbeck) for his immense
skill as an artist, his bold affairs and intrigues, and his un-
limited ego.[50]

With its autobiographical protagonist and themes, the
story reflects Steinbeck's living conditions in Manhattan during this lean and unsure period of his life. William rents an
undistinguished upstairs room with white curtains, brown
walls, and a filled-in fire place framed with grey lavatory
marble. Steinbeck's own flat in Gramercy Park was similarly "up six flights of stairs in the old Parkwood Hotel,"
according to Benson, "and cost seven dollars a week."
Steinbeck friend Bill Black remembers it as a "terrible
room." The young author's only constant companions were
cockroaches and bedbugs, which hid behind grease-stained
pictures hung on the wall.[51]

While valuable for its autobiographical content, Steinbeck's untitled Christmas story contains the flaws and awk-
wardnesses typical of a first draft. Nonetheless, we are
fortunate to have this unpublished story which provides an
early instance of Steinbeck's awareness of America's

dispossessed (the lift operator and prostitute), his scepti-
cism of its commercial values (as manifested in the Metropolitan tower), and his realization that the nonconformist in
America (William alias the young Steinbeck) constantly faces
fear and loneliness. In the next tale, he extends his interest in Manhattan's less fortunate to the ethnically diverse
region around Fourteenth Street on the Lower East Side.

"The White Sister of Fourteenth Street"
(ca. 1924-26)

At the time Steinbeck wrote "The White Sister of Fourteenth Street," the first three words of the story's title
would have been familiar to most readers.[52] Based on Francis Marion Crawford's novel, The White Sister (1909), a silent film rendition starring Lillian Gish and Ronald Coleman
premiered in New York in 1924. Because of the popularity
and fine performance of Lillian Gish, the film was successful
and widely known.[53]

Briefly, the action in Crawford's novel unfolds like
this:

> Angela Chiaromente, heir to a vast Italian estate,
> is left penniless and homeless when her father dies
> and her half-sister, the Marchesa di Mola, destroys
> the will dividing the property between the two daugh-
> ters. Angela's fiance, Giovanni Severini, goes to war
> in Africa, promising marriage on his return. When
> reports of his death arrive, Angela joins [the Con-
> vent of the White Sisters of Santo Giovanni d' Aza].
> Angela's fiance taken prisoner, escapes to Italy and
> there meets Angela, whom he tries to persuade to
> renounce her vows.[54]

At the point of crisis in Crawford's novel, Angela's
dilemma is resolved by a priest, Ippolito Saracinesca, who
promises to obtain a Papal dispensation to release Angela from
her sacred vows and allow her to marry her fiance, Giovanni.
The dramatic, operatic, and film versions of The White Sister,
however, differ from Crawford's novel in the resolution of
the crisis. In these subsequent renditions, the conclusion
is tragic: Angela adheres to her holy pledge, and as a result of the Mount Vesuvius eruption, Giovanni dies.[55]

Steinbeck was perhaps most familiar with this latter denoue-
ment, for the opera version which plays a prominent part in
his short story ends this way.

Steinbeck relies heavily on the opera to lend structure
and meaning to "The White Sister of Fourteenth Street." The
story concerns how young Elsie Grough finds and loses Angelo, the man of her dreams. One evening he takes her to
hear the opera, La Monaca Bianca (The White Sister). Steinbeck's placement of the musical drama in a dilapidated theatre on Fourteenth Street is no coincidence; for sometime between 1924 and 1926 La Monaca Bianca, produced by Clemente
Giglio's Italian Opera Company, played at New York's Fourteenth Street Theatre (105 W. 14th St.), and Steinbeck himself may well have attended a performance.[56] In "The White
Sister of Fourteenth Street" Angelo (also known as "Wappapa," a cool, slick idol of the Lower East Side) undergoes an
emotional metamorphosis. During the final act of the opera,
he bursts into tears. Although Elsie knows little Italian and
cannot share Angelo's excitement, she is astonished by his
transformation. When the curtain falls, Wappapa applauds
wildly, and then flies out of the theatre with Elsie straggling
behind. In the rush they are separated. Elsie runs into
the foyer to seek Wappapa, but too late. He has disappeared.

Since Steinbeck's third-person narrator remains outside
the minds of both characters, the reader can only guess at
Angelo's dissatisfactions with Elsie. This, in part, contributes to the seeming inconclusiveness of the story. The narrator does mention Angelo as one ingredient in Manhattan's
vast melting pot, in which various nationalities are efficiently
blended together. But for Angelo the melting pot apparently
fails. He resists assimilation, perhaps only passively at
first, but after attending the Italian opera his ethnic roots
reassert themselves and his metamorphosis occurs.

Both characters, Angelo and Elsie, appear somewhat
shallow, even moronic. This is less true of Angelo than of
Elsie, for at least the reader sees outward signs of Angelo's
churning emotions during the opera. Obviously, Angelo is
deeply touched by the performance, his emotion confirmed
by his tears. Elsie, on the other hand, shows little evidence
of having deeply felt anything. Not knowing Elsie very well
by the story's end, we feel merely puzzled, rather than
sorry that she is abandoned by Angelo. Thus, while "The

White Sister" comprises a "pretty good attempt at light com-
edy," according to Benson, it is "self-conscious," "slick and
sentimental," and "overdone."[57] The story rates a notch
below Steinbeck's other tales from this period.

"The Nymph and Isobel"
(ca. 1924-26)

Of Steinbeck's four existing Lower Manhattan stories,
"The Nymph and Isobel" most obviously belongs to the "Bowery fiction" sub-genre discussed above.[58] Perhaps with its
conventions in mind, Steinbeck sketches the dark, ominous
towers of an indifferent city. This gloomy backdrop gives
way early in the narrative to Isobel's fantasies of nymphs
and fairylands. In order to escape her miserable surroundings, Isobel conjures up a fantasy so vivid that it displaces
her reality. A defenseless vagrant, Isobel must cope with
an unfriendly city which offers her no shelter, a garment
district sweat shop where she earns only twelve dollars a
week, and an aggressive man who takes advantage of her.
Isobel's story involves her attempted flight from these dis-
mal circumstances.

One sultry evening after toiling all day at Moe Greenberg's shop, Isobel emerges from a subway station pursued
by a square man in a black overcoat. Having nowhere to go,
she reluctantly accompanies him to a small park, dwarfed by
the dark cliffs of nearby buildings. Isobel spots a glimmer-
ing fountain at the center of the park and dips her arms into
its deep pool. She becomes entranced by several diamonds
of light on the surface, when one begins to grow into the
shape of a woman. A nymph-like creature appears and introduces herself as Cyrea. Sensing Isobel's unhappiness,
Cyrea invites her to swim away to a fairyland. Although
the square man whistles for her return, Isobel jumps into
the pool. Cyrea has disappeared. When Isobel begins to
sink, the square man yanks her from the water. He calls
her a fool, and then promises her dry clothes and dinner
in Chinatown.

Like Vinch in "East Third Street," Isobel strives
against great odds towards a better life. Both protagonists
face opposition. Vinch contends with Dominick, Isobel with
the square man. These dark oppressors resemble one

another, as do the two protagonists they tyrannize. Steinbeck chooses apt symbols to represent the victims. A whim-
pering bird dog in "East Third Street" suggests Vinch's lost
courage; the tiny park dwarfed by steep, dark buildings
signifies Isobel's vulnerability to the square man. Dressed
in black, the square man becomes a manifestation of the ugly
metropolis--a walking metaphor of the city.

Steinbeck may have originally set "The Nymph and Isobel" in Southern California, according to Benson, and later
changed the backdrop to Manhattan so that the tale would
conform to the New York theme of his projected volume of
short stories. Benson believes that Steinbeck's nymph is
modeled after a Greek statue in the fountain of the Hill
Street Park in Los Angeles.[59] Whether it originated on the
East or West coast, the tale's urban atmosphere reflects
earlier fictional treatments of the slums. Steinbeck's Isobel
resembles Stephen Crane's protagonist in Maggie, A Girl of
the Streets (1893). Both Isobel and Maggie are poor working girls on Manhattan's Lower East Side. Their living conditions are painfully similar to those described by Jacob Riis'
in How the Other Half Lives (1890). Riis shows how such
working girls often tramped the streets seeking employment,
but found "the only living wages" offered were "the wages
of sin."[60] After long hours sewing garments at Moe Greenberg's shop, Isobel too is tempted by "wages of sin," and
only through her fantasies can she escape. The mystical
habitation which lures Isobel is one of many created by Steinbeck in his early stories. Similar settings and mythic creatures appear in "Adventures in Arcademy" (1924) and Steinbeck's finest published tale of the decade, "The Gifts of
Iban" (1927).

"The Days of Long Marsh"
(ca. 1924-26)

"The Days of Long Marsh" is the only extant story of
this group set in "Steinbeck Country."[61] Lawrence W. Jones
calls it a pathetic tale of an "old hermit attempting to hold
onto the dreams of the past."[62] Yet the overriding theme of
the story is loneliness and the tricks it plays on the lonely
ones. Steinbeck develops this theme with an unusual image,
a row of shiny catsup bottles in which the old recluse stores
his memories.

The tale unfolds in an eerie atmosphere. One frosty
night on Long Marsh a young hunter loses his way and falls
into a pool of icy water. The hermit, hearing his cries,
pulls the hunter to safety and leads him across the marsh
to a small, driftwood hut at the foot of a hill he calls "Lomita." Inside the hut are some unusual furnishings, including a shelf lined with the brightly polished catsup bottles.
When the old man mentions his deceased wife, Nellie, who
has become a voice on the marsh calling him night after night,
the hunter begins to question his host's sanity. Yet strang-
er occurrences are to come: the old man reaches for a catsup bottle from the shelf--Monday, the first of his "days" of
Long Marsh. Monday was before everything, he says, even
before his wife, Nellie. The second bottle is Tuesday, the
best day of all because of the white house and Nellie. The
third bottle is Wednesday, reminding the old man of Nellie's
tragic death. The next, Thursday, is the day the white
house burned. The hermit invites the hunter to stay and
put some of his own "days" on the shelf, but his guest tact-
fully declines. The departing hunter sloshes through the
greying night, thinking about his lonely host's "days" of
Long Marsh.

In terms of subject matter, "The Days of Long Marsh"
is an unusual addition to the Steinbeck canon, even considering that it takes place in "Steinbeck Country," involves pro-
totypic Steinbeck characters, and suggests the recurrent
Steinbeck theme of loneliness. No precedent for the row of
shiny catsup bottles exists in Steinbeck's earlier fiction nor
does such a device turn up in his later works. Amasa Miller provides a clue to the origin of these polished bottles.
Miller recalls an incident involving himself, Steinbeck, and
Stanford teacher/story writer Elizabeth (E.C.A.) Smith.
Smith (pseudonym, John Breck) took an interest in Steinbeck, and after reading one of his stories, "A Lady in Infra-
Red" (kernel of Cup of Gold), summoned him to her home.
Her encouragement and frank criticism of the story prompted
Steinbeck to adopt Smith as a confidante and mentor for the
remainder of the spring term, 1925. Miller, who sometimes
accompanied Steinbeck to Smith's residence, says that one
time John read to Smith and him "at her apartment in Palo
Alto, a story about a succession of girl friends kept in separate bottles."63 While the manuscript of this piece has
never turned up, its unique subject matter reappears somewhat altered in "The Days of Long Marsh."

One identifying trait of Steinbeck's artistry in "The
Days of Long Marsh" is its abundance of plant and animal
imagery. Steinbeck refers to the marsh recluse as if he
were a giant bird flailing his wings. Similarly, the old man's
laughter is made to sound like the cackling of a hen or
goose; his nose projects a shadow on the wall which looks
like a tremendous beak. Other animal images include drakes,
coyotes, coons, serpents, and geese; plant imagery consists
of flowers and other vegetation of infinite variety: lupin,
everlastings, and lavender, as well as cranberries, potatoes,
cabbages, ivy, and tules.

"The Days of Long Marsh" is perhaps Steinbeck's best
unpublished story of this period. Its dramatic intensity and
haunting conclusion suggest that Steinbeck had outgrown the
shallow, one-dimensional characters and tenuous plots of his
earlier stories. Moreover, the setting of "Long Marsh" shows
Steinbeck once again depicting the territory he knew best.
"Lomita" (which in Spanish means low, broad hill) is modeled
after Castroville, a coastal town in "Steinbeck Country"
nestled at the mouth of the Salinas River. We will see this
setting again in the later story, "Johnny Bear" (1934).

"The Nail"
(ca. 1924-26)

Taking us far from his native region, in "The Nail"
Steinbeck dramatizes the Old Testament story of Sisera and
Jael.[64] Since he borrows the story directly from the book
of Judges, its plot can be summarized briefly: Beneath
Mount Tabor in the hot desert sand of Canaan, Sisera--
commander of King Jabin's forces--crawls wearily dragging
his wounded leg, recently struck by a Hebrew arrow. His
armour is broken, his helmet and sword lost. He recalls
how Hebrews defeated and killed his comrades, and defiled
their bodies with spittle. Now Sisera must elude his enemies or die. He spots a small tent and crawls toward it for
safety. Inside, he is greeted cautiously by Jael, wife of
Heber--a Jew friendly to Canaanite King Jabin. When Sisera
confides in her that he has killed the Hebrew chieftain who
wounded his leg, Jael recognizes this chieftain as her son.
She encourages Sisera to sleep and then pulls an iron tent
nail from the ground. Pausing momentarily over the slum-
bering Sisera, she drives it into his head.

"The Nail" is similar to other Old Testament dramatiza-
tions by popular writers of the 1920s. Donn Byrne, a favorite of Steinbeck, retells the story of Sampson and Delilah in
his collection, The Changeling and Other Stories (1923).
Donn Byrne's tale, "Delilah, Now It Was Dusk," is like Steinbeck's "The Nail" in several ways: both stories are drawn
from Judges; both involve a man and a woman of opposing
nations (the Israelites versus the Canaanites and Philistines);
and both depict how the man takes the woman into his confidence, and then is betrayed by her. Benson suggests that
Steinbeck may also have been influenced by Donn Byrne's
Brother Saul (1927).[65]

    Although Steinbeck takes his story of Sisera and Jael
directly from the Bible, he makes some subtle and interesting changes. The most obvious alteration concerns the point
of view. While both versions are written in the third-person,
Steinbeck funnels the events through Sisera's eyes, rather
than through Jael's (as in Judges). Consequently, Steinbeck's Sisera becomes a more sympathetic figure, especially
in light of Jael's cunning execution of him. This is not the
case in the original, where God is on the side of the Israelites: hence Jael, a Hebrew, naturally becomes the story's
heroine, while Sisera, a Canaanite, the story's villain. Perhaps this change in focus reflects Steinbeck's life-long dis-
trust of crusaders who justify acts of destruction in the name
of God, or communism, or anything else. Sisera and his
Canaanite people are victims of an onslaught by the Israelites who believe God has ordained them to exterminate Sisera's pagan nation. Benson suggests Steinbeck's subtle
reversal of the biblical message shows "that the Canaanites'
way of life was richer and far more beautiful than the ster-
ile, deadly fanaticism" of their opponents.[66]

    In addition to this shift in emphasis achieved by focus-
ing on Sisera rather than Jael, Steinbeck makes several other
changes from the Old Testament story. The desert setting,
barely mentioned in Judges, Steinbeck elaborates on in great
detail. He emphasizes the effect on Sisera of the blazing-hot
sun, and the pitiful sight of a wounded man crawling on the
scorching desert. In the biblical text, no mention is made
of the wound on Sisera's leg; in fact, he walks freely into
Jael's tent. In addition, no son of Jael fires the arrow which
makes the wound. Jael's son--a chieftain of the people of
Zebulun--seems to be Steinbeck's embellishment.

These small changes made by Steinbeck lead to a more
significant difference between the two texts. In Judges,
Jael is applauded for her allegiance to the Hebrew cause; by
killing Sisera--a national enemy--she becomes a true daughter
of Israel. Yet in Steinbeck's adaptation, Jael drives a tent
spike into Sisera's head primarily to revenge the death of
her son. Steinbeck's Jael behaves differently in other ways
as well. She plays an active role in the Old Testament
story: through a prophecy of Debora (Judges iv.1), Sisera
is to be delivered into her hands. Thus, instead of being
surprised by the Canaanite as Steinbeck describes the episode, in the biblical story Jael emerges from her tent to
greet Sisera and invite him in. Jael's murder in the original
version seems to be premeditated and ordained by God. Yet
Steinbeck's Jael is less certain as to how she should behave
toward a wounded enemy of her nation. In fact, she sympa-
thizes with the Canaanites when Sisera describes the havoc
wreaked on them by the Hebrews. Thus, Steinbeck makes
Jael a more human character--subject to feelings of pity,
guilt, and, most importantly, revenge.

Like other early Steinbeck stories, "The Nail" abounds
with colorful images. Reflecting the scorching heat of the
desert, Steinbeck repeats the imagery of gold, yellow, brown,
and red. Suggesting the implements of war, he mentions
such metals as brass, bronze, and iron. The most important
of these images is Jael's weapon, a tent nail. This sharp
spike of untarnished iron becomes the focus of the story.
It is perhaps ironic that while all the Israelite swords,
spears, and arrows of battle miss their fatal mark on Sisera,
a single tent nail wielded by Jael causes his downfall. Although "The Nail" is one of Steinbeck's most artistically refined stories of the 1920s, his best of the decade--"The Gifts
of Iban"--found its way into print early in 1927.

"THE GIFTS OF IBAN"
(1927)

The debut of "The Gifts of Iban" marked several milestones in Steinbeck's career: It was his first story accepted
by a national publication. Calling it a "delightful fantasy,"
editor Gerry Fitzgerald selected Steinbeck's tale for the pre-
miere issue of the short-lived Smoker's Companion magazine

(March, 1927). The story was also the first published work
in which Steinbeck used a pseudonym. He took the nom de
plume, "John Stern," since "he did not like the name of the
magazine, and did not want to be associated with it."[67] Finally, "The Gifts of Iban" was the first piece for which
Steinbeck earned money. Although the sale netted him only
fifteen dollars, it no doubt revived his hopes for succeeding
as a writer.[68] Despite these three milestones, texts of the
story are scarce. It has never been reprinted, and only a
few copies of the magazine in which the original appeared
have survived.

"The Gifts of Iban" shares with Steinbeck's other early
fiction the theme of rejection, especially women rejecting
their male suitors. Just as Pedro in "Fingers of Cloud" is
abandoned by his new bride, Gertie, and Henry Morgan in
Cup of Gold (1929) is snubbed by the beautiful La Santa
Roja, Iban loses the woman of his dreams. In a magical
forest of scarlet trees and tiny houses carved of ivory, Iban
falls in love with the angelic, winged Cantha. He proposes
to her, promising Cantha "gifts" of golden sunlight, silver
moonbeams, and sweet melodies. But Iban's evanescent gifts
pale in comparison to the earthly gold and silver of rival
suitor, Glump, king of the Gnomes. Against her mother's
urging, Cantha refuses Glump and marries Iban. Later,
when she decides that Iban's gifts are valueless, Cantha
changes her mind. She walks out on him, regretting her
lost chance to wed the wealthy Glump and become queen of
the Gnomes. As she disappears into the forest, Iban lies
shivering on the ground, heartbroken.

As does "Adventures in Arcademy," Steinbeck's third
published story reveals the influence of American novelist,
James Branch Cabell. The setting and characters of "The
Gifts of Iban" are nearly identical to those in chapters three
and four of Cabell's Jurgen (1922). Cabell's backdrop,
"The Garden between Dawn and Sunrise," is a mystical garden visible only "in the brief interval between dawn and
sunrise."[69] Similarly, Steinbeck's "brightly colored" forest
resembles "a half-remembered dream" (p. 18), a twilight
world where the line between reality and fantasy blurs.
Steinbeck's characters, too, find their counterparts in Cabell's Jurgen. Iban, Cantha, and Glump resemble Cabell's
Jurgen, Dorothy la Desiree, and Heitman Michael, respec-
tively. And Iban manifests a primary trait of Cabellian

heroes--to yearn for "a paragon of beautiful womanhood,"
who eventually rejects him. 70

    Steinbeck, himself, underwent a disappointment similar
to Iban's. Before completing "Gifts," he had a fleeting romance in New York City with aspiring actress, Mary Ardeth.
Steinbeck quickly fell in love and anticipated their marrying
after he published his first book. But then Ardeth announced ...

> She had no intention of starting married life with
> someone whose ambitions did not include the achieve-
> ment of financial security. If he were to give up
> his foolish writing ambition and accept [some form
> of stable employment], she would look with more
> favor on his idea of marriage. 71

    Ardeth abruptly left Steinbeck in New York for her
home in Chicago. Soon after she delivered the final blow:
a letter explaining she had become engaged to a banker.
Perhaps Steinbeck's unsuccessful suit for Mary Ardeth en-
tered his thoughts as he crafted the plot of "Gifts." Steinbeck may have originally intended the story as a parable on
"the eternal struggle between the sexes," but when he rewrote it at Fallen Leaf Lake in the Sierra Mountains during
summer, 1926, he changed it into a "cautionary tale for his
friend [Dook Sheffield] on the threats that marriage poses
to masculine dreams and ambitions." 72

    Aside from its biographical interest, "The Gifts of
Iban" shows that Steinbeck had developed a new maturity of
tone and style, and a greater degree of control over plotting
and characterization. He was able to temper his stylistic
flourishes of earlier stories, and abandon his sometimes
ridiculing tone for one of empathy and compassion. Thus,
Iban and Cantha emerge as round, believable characters,
revealing human emotions noticeably missing in previous
Steinbeck characters. Although Cantha favors Iban's proposal, we watch her mother's cautions about the penniless
bard change her mind. When Cantha finally rejects Iban,
her sudden turnabout is convincing. Iban's forlornness is
equally believable, and further demonstrates Steinbeck's
ability to create characters of feeling with whom the reader
can identify. Thus, "The Gifts of Iban" brings to a close
Steinbeck's apprenticeship as a story writer. When Smoker's

<u>Companion</u> editor Fitzgerald accepted the story for publication, he was acknowledging the arrival of a new and promising talent among writers of short fiction.

Chapter Two

THE PASTURES OF HEAVEN (1932)

Introduction

With the publication of "The Gifts of Iban" (1927), Steinbeck's apprenticeship as a story writer came to an end. He had developed a new maturity of tone and style and a greater degree of control over plotting and characterization. Nonetheless, when "Gifts" appeared, Steinbeck had yet to rediscover the geographic region and its inhabitants that would act as a catalyst for his special genius. In The Pastures of Heaven, he draws upon these materials which were indigenous to his native land--real people, places, and incidents.[1] In a May, 1931 letter to Mavis McIntosh, Steinbeck explains:

> There is, about twelve miles from Monterey, a valley in the hills called Corral de Tierra. Because I am using its people I have named it Las Pasturas del Cielo. The valley was for years known as the happy valley because of the unique harmony which existed among its twenty families. About ten years ago a new family moved in on one of the ranches. They were ordinary people, ill-educated but honest and as kindly as any. In fact, in their whole history I cannot find that they have committed a really malicious act nor an act which was not dictated by honorable expediency or out-and-out altruism. But about the Morans ["Munroes" in Pastures] there was a flavor of evil. Everyone they came in contact with was injured. Every place they went dissension sprang up. There have been two murders, a suicide, many quarrels and a great deal of unhappiness in the Pastures of Heaven, and all of these

29

things can be traced directly to the influence of the
Morans.[2]

The Munroe "curse," as Steinbeck calls it, seemingly
turns the Pastures into an unhappy valley. Although they
seldom directly cause their neighbors' misfortunes, in every
story the Munroes precipitate a final disaster that might have
occurred even without their intrusion. "The apparent tran-
quility of each resident," according to Joseph Fontenrose, is
"founded on an unhealthy adjustment, either an evasion of
reality or an unrealizable dream." In one sense, what Bert
Munroe and his family provide for Pastures residents is a
"moment of truth," when they must see their "unhealthy adjustment" for what it is.[3]

Of the twenty families mentioned in Steinbeck's letter
about The Pastures of Heaven, he examines the Munroe's effect on nine in as many interrelated stories. Critics through
the years have argued over the generic form of these nine
tales gathered in one volume. Early reviews unabashedly call
the Pastures a collection of short fiction; one review in the
October 29, 1932, New York Evening Post is typical: "This
book is really a series of short stories, rather than a novel."[4] Later critics arrived at similar conclusions. In The
Novels of John Steinbeck (1939), Harry Thornton Moore says:
"The Pastures of Heaven is not strictly a novel, though in
categorizing Steinbeck's work we treat it as such: it is really a group of loosely connected stories that are given a suggestion of unity by an artificial frame."[5] Warren French appropriately calls the work a "short-story cycle" whose separate narratives are related to one another, yet autonomous.[6]
French borrows the term from Forrest L. Ingram's Representative Short-Story Cycles of the Twentieth Century (1971).

While not identical in form to collections like The Long
Valley (1938), Steinbeck's Pastures of Heaven can equally
well be approached as a collection. Steinbeck himself says
of its stories: "each one [is] complete in itself, having its
rise, climax, and ending."[7] It is no surprise, then, that he
sold two tales from the collection separately and each was
published as an autonomous story. Although Pastures is divided into twelve chapters, the prologue (Ch. I) and epilogue
(Ch. XII) contain only brief sketches intended to set the
tone of the volume and provide a frame of reference. Chapter Two similarly introduces the Battle Farm and the Munroe

family who eventually settle in it. Thus, our discussion begins with the first complete story, "Shark Wicks" (Ch. III).

"Shark Wicks"
(Ch. III)

Steinbeck placed the Shark Wicks story first before all
other tales in The Pastures of Heaven for good reason. It
features a complex, two-tiered plot which gradually reveals
Shark's twin obsessions: his pretended wealth and his
daughter's chastity. Shark, his wife, Katherine, and daughter, Alice, live on a small peach farm in the Pastures. When
Jimmie Munroe moves to the idyllic valley, stories about his
infamous past spread quickly. Shark instructs Alice never to
talk to Jimmie; but Alice does not heed her father's warning.
Once when Shark goes away to a funeral, Katherine takes
her daughter to a school dance. Jimmie coaxes Alice onto the
floor and then rushes her outside under the willow trees.
When T.B. Allen, proprietor of the Pastures general store,
tells Shark about the episode, he sets out for the Munroe
home with a rifle. Allen informs the deputy sheriff, and
Wicks is arrested. Because of Shark's reputed fortune, Bert
Munroe, Jimmie's father, insists on a ten-thousand dollar
bond, forcing Shark to disclose that he has no money. He
returns home a broken man, his two greatest pleasures in
life having been lost. Although Shark's fears about his
daughter's chastity prove unfounded, the Wicks soon move
away from their acreage in the Pastures.

The farm the Wicks leave behind says volumes about
Shark's miserly character, particularly his zeal for shrewd
"investments" and contrasting neglect of his family. Their
brown farmhouse is "the only unbeautiful thing on the farm."
Its debris-strewn yard, where not a single flower grows,
suggests that Shark ignores his family. For although he
irrigates his orchard which turns a profit, he sees "no reason for wasting good water around the house." Hence, instead of colorful floral patterns surrounding the dwelling,
there are only "old sacks, with papers, bits of broken glass
and tangles of baling wire." In contrast, Shark maintains
his peach orchard immaculately, for it is a visible reminder
to the people of the valley of his business acumen.[8]

Shark's physical appearance and behavior also reveal

the kind of person he is. His "blunt, brown face and small,
cold eyes" suggest a tightfisted, calculating man who is
"never so happy as when he could force a few cents more out
of his peaches than his neighbors did" (p. 26). Steinbeck
carefully sketches other characters, as well. Alice Wicks and
Jimmie Munroe are recognizable types: the stereotyped teenage beauty and the high school cassanova. T.B. Allen, who
appears in four tales, plays a significant role by telling
Shark about Alice's encounter with Jimmie and then calling
the deputy to intercept Shark.

The most surprising character is Shark's usually quiet
wife, Katherine. Her brief and unexpected metamorphosis
marks an early instance in Steinbeck's fiction of the neglected
wife's sudden rise to power, and then her sudden decline.[9]
Steinbeck portrays Katherine Mullock (her maiden name) as a
homely, but vigorous young bride. Yet, "[a]fter her marriage
she lost her vigour and her freshness as a flower does once
it has received pollen" (p. 30). For most of the story, she
busies herself with domestic chores, especially tending her
garden, while Shark works in the peach orchard.

Then at mid-point in the narrative she explodes at her
husband's nagging inquiries about Alice's chastity: " 'You're
a dirty, suspicious skunk,' she told him. 'You get out of
here! And if you ever talk about it again, I'll--I'll go away' "
(p. 37). Katherine's outburst astonishes Shark, but it
doesn't frighten or change him. Yet his wife's inner strength
quietly grows.

Katherine finally rebels against her husband's meddling
when she takes Alice to a school dance in Shark's absence.
" 'We will go,' " she exclaims, as if she had just overcome a
tremendous obstacle. "She felt very brave to be encourag-
ing Shark's unease" (p. 44). Katherine's strength grows,
crests, and then diminishes at the end of the story. She is
at the height of her power when Shark returns home down-
cast after publicly revealing his bogus wealth. Katherine
watches Shark approach from the vegetable garden and is
"bitterly glad of the slump of his shoulders and of his head's
weak carriage" (p. 53). Suddenly a surge of energy infuses
Katherine. A "strong instinct" sets her to stroking her husband's forehead, as he confesses the sham of his non-existent
wealth. As Shark laments, Katherine's

great genius continued to grow in her. She felt
larger than the world.... Suddenly the genius in
Katherine became power and the power gushed in
her body and flooded her.... In this moment she
was a goddess, a singer of destiny (p. 55).

Shark, now nearly revived by his wife's ministrations,
notices how beautiful she is and "as he looked her genius
passed into him" (p. 56). Katherine becomes frightened
when the power leaves her. Her energy seems to funnel
directly into her husband as it drains out of her. Katherine, who experiences this sudden flow and ebb of power,
foreshadows Elisa Allen in "The Chrysanthemums" (1937).
Both become what Marilyn L. Mitchell calls Steinbeck's "strong
women," taking on strengths normally associated with men,
but lacking in their own husbands.[10]

The surprising metamorphosis of Katherine Wicks is one
of the many reasons why the Shark Wicks story deserves the
first position among other tales in The Pastures of Heaven.
Its complex, double plot, credible characterization, and vivid
setting make the narrative one of the finest in the collection.
Steinbeck no doubt realized its technical excellence and therefore placed it first in the volume.

"Tularecito"
(Ch. IV)

The main attraction of Steinbeck's second tale in The
Pastures of Heaven is a frog-like young boy named "Tularecito." Richard Astro calls him the first sub-normal character in Steinbeck's fiction, and the prototype for Lennie Small
in Of Mice and Men (1937).[11] The Tularecito story can also
be considered a forerunner of "Johnny Bear" (1937), another
tale in which Steinbeck shapes the narrative around a bizarre,
animal-like character.

Tularecito, whose name in Spanish means "little frog,"
has an appropriately shaped body: "short, chubby arms,
and long loose-jointed legs" (p. 59). A foundling who grows
up on the farm of Franklin Gomez, "Little Frog" enjoys a
serene youth until he is compelled to attend the Pastures
school. Already he has developed a powerful body and a
talent for carving little animals from sandstone; yet if anyone

handles carelessly or destroys these animals, Tularecito becomes violent. At school, this unusual boy evidences a new talent: he can draw animals on the blackboard as expertly as he can carve them. But once when several children begin to erase these creatures, Tularecito flies into a rage. Reinforcing his love for little animals, Tularecito's teacher encourages him to believe in gnomes, and one night he digs for them in Bert Munroe's orchard. The next morning when Munroe, inspecting a coyote trap, finds the hole and begins to fill it in, Tularecito crowns him with a shovel. Jimmie Munroe discovers his father lying by the hole and calls several nighbors who subdue Tularecito. A medical board rules that he should be committed to an asylum for the criminal insane.

Although the Munroe "curse" theme in Pastures requires at least one Munroe to appear in every story, the ending of "Tularecito" set in the Munroe orchard seems contrived. Neither the Munroe family nor their farm is mentioned anywhere in the tale except at its very end. As Howard Levant says: "[Tularecito] could have dug in anyone's orchard. The fact that he digs in Bert's orchard is too overtly accidental to have much convincing fictional significance."[12]

One possible link between Tularecito and the Munroes is the coyote trap that Bert plans to inspect when he comes upon the large pit dug by the "Little Frog." Previously, Franklin Gomez has called Tularecito "Coyote," for he saw in the "boy's face that ancient wisdom one finds in the face of a coyote" (p. 59). That Bert Munroe's errand concerns a coyote trap, therefore, may have significance. Even so, this connection between Tularecito and the Munroes is tenuous at best, and does not prepare the reader for the abrupt appearance of Bert and Jimmie at the story's end.

Other questions arise over the theme of the story. Peter Lisca suggests society's intrusion into the individual's adjustment as a possible theme, but the tale can also be seen as the purely naturalistic downfall of an animal-like foundling who lives at variance with society's conventions. Tularecito is destined to go astray, regardless of the assistance he receives from well-meaning friends. The people of the valley cannot cope with him, so they have him put away.[13]

Two notable minor characters in the story are Tularecito's school teachers, Miss Martin and Molly Morgan. When
taken together, their names resemble that of Steinbeck's aunt
and one-time resident of the Corral de Tierra, Molly Martin.
As a boy Steinbeck had visited his aunt and listened to stories about "the local lore of the isolated valley."[14] Who recounted these tales to Steinbeck is not absolutely certain, but
Richard Astro reveals that the raconteur may have been a
neighbor of Molly Martin, Beth Ingels. Later Miss Ingels
was to accuse Steinbeck of stealing some of the Pastures
stories from her.[15]

The young teacher in the Tularecito story, Molly Morgan, recalls Steinbeck's own mother, Olive Hamilton Steinbeck, who was also a school teacher. Molly plays a significant role in three tales--one devoted entirely to herself (Ch.
VIII), the Junius Maltby tale (Ch. VI), and here in "Tularecito" (Ch. IV). Her actions in the present story are particularly important since she motivates Tularecito to dig with a
shovel for gnomes, and as a result he winds up in an insane
asylum. Molly's provoking the half-witted young boy is irresponsible, given its ultimate effect upon him. Compared
to her actions in the two other tales, Molly's behavior in this
story is oddly intrusive. She reveals to Tularecito her philosophy of life, which hinges on man's deep desire to express
himself--to carve his initials in the white cliffs of time: " 'to
leave some record of himself, a proof, perhaps, that he has
really existed. He leaves his proof on wood, on stone or on
the lives of other people' " (p. 69). Proving her existence by
influencing others may be what Molly Morgan has in mind
when she encourages the "Little Frog" to believe in the creatures of fairy tales. For whatever reason, Molly inadvertent-
ly precipitates the arrest and ultimate confinement of Tularecito. Bert Munroe, by comparison, is merely a bystander
who gets in the way when "Little Frog" follows Miss Morgan's instructions to their logical conclusion. From this
results the story's chief structural problem.

"Helen Van Deventer"
(Ch. V)

The next tale features two women, a mother and daughter, who are mentally deranged. Helen Van Deventer has the

morbid need to endure tragedy. Her daughter, Hilda, hallu-
cinates, tells enormous lies, and explodes into fits of rage.
Throughout the story, Hilda's mental aberrations are clearly
evident; yet her mother's perhaps worse sickness is only
slowly revealed.

When Helen Van Deventer loses her husband, Hubert,
in a hunting accident six months after their wedding, she
has him stuffed and mounted in their library. Soon their
only child is born mentally ill. A physician suggests that
the daughter, Hilda, be committed to a hospital for the insane, but Helen refuses. She moves from San Francisco to
a beautifully landscaped new home in the Pastures, where
she again enshrines her husband in a memorial room. Dis-
liking the paradisal valley, Hilda becomes angry and strikes
her mother. Helen's Chinese cook locks the screaming girl
in her room, whose windows are fortified with oak bars.
Bert Munroe learns of his new neighbors and decides to wel-
come them. When he arrives at the Deventer's, he hears
Hilda shrieking at her window. Hilda claims she is being
starved and proposes marriage to Munroe in order to escape.
When Munroe knocks at the front door to check Hilda's story,
he is rebuffed by the cook. Eventually, Hilda flees and is
pursued by her mother, carrying a shotgun. Later, the Pastures coroner rules Hilda's gunshot death a suicide.

Although Munroe intrudes very late in the story, Steinbeck prepares for his precipitous visit with two earlier scenes.
In the first, Bert tells T.B. Allen about the "'big thick oak'"
bars on the windows of the new house (p. 87). In the second, Bert suggests to his wife that he may call on their new
neighbors "'and see if they need anything'" (p. 89). Mrs.
Munroe protests that Bert is merely curious, rather than concerned. Slightly miffed, he ventures toward the Van Deventer place anyway.

In addition to this central action featuring Helen and
Hilda Van Deventer and the Munroes, another significant
thread in the plot involves Helen's memories of her deceased
husband, Hubert. Emerging as flashbacks in Helen's mind,
this thread provides essential background information, especially Helen's knowledge of guns and how to use them.
Steinbeck subtly prepares the way for Hilda's murder by describing Helen's first experience firing a shotgun under Hubert's watchful eye. She recalls Hubert's admonition: "'I

don't want you ever to shoot at a still target--ever. It is a
poor sportsman who will shoot a resting bird'" (p. 97).

Even though Steinbeck omits the actual kill, it is adequately suggested by this reminiscence. But this is only
one of many flashbacks to Helen's brief marriage and her life
as a sportsman's widow. These flashbacks taken together
reveal the hidden truth about her demented mind. First we
learn how Hubert shot himself accidentally on a hunting trip
and requested that Helen have him stuffed and mounted in
the library of their home. Thereafter, for many years Helen
holds frequent vigils in the room, evoking Hubert's image.
The narrator emphasizes that during these habitual exercises
Helen can actually reconstruct her husband's body. In this
way she extends the period of her mourning for more than
a decade, until moving to the Pastures of Heaven. Although
in her new home Helen builds a room resembling a hunting
lodge to honor her husband, she finds that she can no longer
conjure up his image: "He was gone, completely gone....
Helen put her hands to her face and cried, for the peace
had come back, and the bursting expectancy" (p. 100).

Helen for the first time in fourteen years comes out of
mourning. She releases Hubert from her memory. But the
narrator tells us in the first paragraph that Helen needs
tragedy in her life--she has grown accustomed to it and
loves to wear a "'hair shirt'" (p. 86). Thus, what might be
a relief for most widows is not for Helen. After a momentary
exuberance, she senses something is missing. Where tragedy
once filled her life is now a void. Just minutes later, Helen
reaches for a shotgun. Her target is Hilda. Helen always
has needed to mourn--with her memory of Hubert vanished,
now she must mourn her daughter.

Crucial to our understanding of Helen's sickness is her
physician, Dr. Phillips. Through the physician Steinbeck
demonstrates that Helen is not only disturbed, but also insecure and selfish. Twice Dr. Phillips advises Helen to take
her daughter to a specialist--a psychiatrist. "'Hilda is not
completely well in her mind,'" he tells her (p. 80). Both
times Helen refuses. Finally, at the story's end, Dr. Phillips
reappears--this time to ease Helen's grief and to provide medical opinion on the cause of Hilda's death. His statements
are inconclusive, and hence the murder is ruled a suicide.
Yet Dr. Phillips' most important function in this final scene

is to witness Helen's "severe, her almost savage mourning"
(p. 102). The doctor tells her, "'You look as though you
were going to an execution'" (p. 103).

These three timely appearances by Dr. Phillips, along
with the several flashbacks to Helen's marriage with Hubert,
all add up to an intricately constructed plot. The tragic
conclusion is subtly foreshadowed and each event clearly
leads to another with a causal, almost cumulative effect.
Dramatic intensity builds as it becomes likely that Hilda is
headed for an unfortunate end. Steinbeck relieves this intensity with occasional flashbacks to Hubert's hunting jun-
kets, his accidental death, and Helen's morbid response to
it. Given these strengths, the Van Deventer narrative is
another tale, like "Shark Wicks," which can stand on its own
merits as an autonomous short story.

"Junius Maltby"
(Ch. VI)

Probably the most highly praised chapter in The
Pastures of Heaven is the Junius Maltby story. Acclaimed
by some critics as the only tale entirely reflective of Steinbeck's intended theme and structure for the volume as a
whole, this episodic narrative generally deserves the praise
it has received. Perhaps as testimony to the story's merit,
it was published separately as an illustrated monograph of
370 copies entitled, Nothing So Monstrous (1936).[16]

The tale begins in San Francisco. When fog from the
bay hinders Junius Maltby's recovery from a lung illness,
his doctor encourages him to move to a warm, dry climate.
Maltby moves to the Pastures and boards on the farm of Mrs.
Quaker, a widow whom he eventually marries. Although his
health improves, Maltby proves a lazy farm hand. When a
son, Robbie, is born, the mother dies in childbirth. Robbie
grows up in bare feet and torn overalls, while his father
teaches him the pleasures of nature, leisure, and contempla-
tion. In school, Robbie's classmates tease him about his
shabby clothing. Nonetheless, he soon wins their affection
with his natural charm, maturity, and knowledge of many
outdoor games his father has taught him. But this does not
appease the people of the valley, especially the Munroes, who
scorn the Maltbys' carefree lifestyle. Thus when the school

board makes its yearly visit to the Pastures school, Mrs.
Munroe--against the teacher's wishes--hands Robbie a pack-
age containing new shirts and overalls; embarrassed, Robbie
drops the clothing and runs. After this incident, the Maltbys leave the valley for San Francisco so that Junius can
earn money to buy Robbie better clothes.[17]

    Richard F. Peterson contends that the Junius Maltby
story "best reveals the basic conflict between the life style
of the Munroes and the simple, dream-like existence of the
individuals whose lives are changed by their contact with
the Munroes." Peterson suggests that the dominant theme
of The Pastures of Heaven involves middle-class respectability (the Munroes) and its triumph over the happy and sometimes non-conformist people of the valley (such as Maltby).
Junius exemplifies the kind of happy-go-lucky eccentric that
the people of the valley fear and revile. And as Peterson
points out, Junius and his son, Robbie, remain blissfully
ignorant of their neighbors' disapproval until the advent of
the Munroes. Then they become latter-day Adams, chased
out of Eden by the meddling Mrs. Munroe.[18]

    Along with its thematic appropriateness, "Junius Malt-
by" also contains a generally well-designed plot. However,
we may detect one structural flaw. Midway through the narrative, after Robbie has proven himself to be the undisputed
"king of the school yard" (p. 98) and the sole inventor and
arbitrator of all outdoor games, Steinbeck introduces the re-
dundant "spy game" episode, which constitutes a detour from
the central action. Robbie, deciding to focus his spying activities on the Japanese, organizes a school-wide pact, the
B.A.S.S.F.E.A.J. (Boy's Auxiliary Secret Service for Espi-
onage Against the Japanese) (p. 123). In this spy sketch
Steinbeck introduces a new set of characters who briefly
command our attention and then disappear. The reader becomes absorbed in Takaski Kato, the lead character in the
sketch who overshadows Robbie. And Robbie, himself, begins to behave differently.

    Randall R. Mawer contends that Robbie's behavior
changes because he takes on the role of a Munroe, as a
"leveler and persecutor."[19] Actually, Robbie seems out of
character in this episode not because he becomes a Munroe,
but because he reenacts a real event of Steinbeck's own
youth. Nelson Valjean explains that Steinbeck as a boy in

Salinas dreamed up the B.A.S.S.F.E.A.J. and took the lead-
ership role Robbie plays in the story. The episode in the
Maltby tale, in fact, is nearly a verbatim account of how the
incident actually occurred. The Japanese boy who partici-
pated in the real "Boys' Auxiliary" was Takaski Kato, the
name Steinbeck uses in the sketch. The only difference between Steinbeck's childhood spy game and the one he recounted in the story is that the first meeting of the real
B.A.S.S.F.E.A.J. took place in a Salinas barn, rather than
on a school yard.[20] The fact that the sketch is autobiographical gives ample reason for the noticeable change in
Robbie's character.

Despite this structural flaw, the Junius Maltby story
is no doubt the most appealing in the collection, perhaps because the protagonists are basically admirable people. Junius
and Robbie Maltby display none of the psychological
aberrations of most characters in The Pastures of Heaven.
While we may be reluctant to identify with Tularecito or Helen
Van Deventer, we can happily see ourselves sitting on the
Maltbys' sycamore limb dangling our toes in the cool stream
below. Junius is a lazy, but good man; Robbie is a bright
and imaginative young boy; the Maltbys are likeable "drop-
outs" from society who seem to take their cue from Henry
David Thoreau--they reject the life of quiet desperation of
their neighbors, and rather engage in nobler enterprises as
contemplating the Parthenon under the shade of a sycamore
tree.

The clothing worn by the Maltbys during the story
symbolizes their change in condition from "natural" to artificial men. On the Maltby farm neither Junius nor Robbie
wears shoes, and both don tattered shirts with collars
ripped-off and pants torn out at the knees. This scraggly
attire represents the Maltbys at their happiest. When Mrs.
Munroe gives Robbie new, "respectable" clothing, the Maltbys' Edenic world begins to crumble. Upon their departure
from the Pastures, Junius and Robbie display the append-
ages of artificial man--"cheap new clothes" (p. 138), incon-
venient and uncomfortable. Miss Morgan barely recognizes
them as these symbols of their new life have so altered their
appearance. Thus, their transformation from natural to artificial men is complete.

"The Lopez Sisters"
(Ch. VII)

The tale of Rosa and Maria Lopez is another in which,
like "Tularecito," the Munroes again turn up at the penultimate
moment and indirectly reverse the fortunes of their unsuspecting victims. Rosa and Maria are plump, jolly sisters
who inherit forty acres of rocky hillside--but no money--
from their deceased father. To support themselves, the
sisters decide to sell enchiladas. Business develops slowly,
until one day Rosa gives herself to a customer. Maria also
adopts this practice, and sales boom. The sisters remain
devoutly religious, and never accept money directly for their
"encouragements." Once when Maria is driving into Monterey
for supplies, she gives a lift to an ape-like man named Allen
Hueneker. Bert Munroe sees Hueneker riding with her and
jokingly tells Hueneker's jealous wife that her husband is
running off with Maria. Later the sheriff visits the Lopez
sisters with a complaint that the Lopez girls are running a
"bad house." They must either close their doors or face
arrest. Perplexed by this decision, the sisters move to San
Francisco and become prostitutes.

The motivation behind Bert Munroe's practical joke on
Allen Hueneker, which ultimately ruins the Lopez sisters, is
difficult to imagine. This quick, easy solution imposed on
the story leaves unanswered the most challenging questions
raised by the Lopez sisters' unconventional behavior. The
narrative's conclusion may seem ill-fitting because it was
originally part of a Webster F. Street play, "The Green
Lady," the kernel of Steinbeck's To A God Unknown (1933).
Steinbeck apparently decided not to use the Lopez episode in
that book, and instead revised it for The Pastures of Heav-
en.[21] Besides its implausible ending, the tale is only half
as long as most of the other stories in the collection and the
setting does not reflect the paradisal atmosphere established
in the early chapters of Pastures. Steinbeck places the
Lopez sisters' clapboard shack on "starved soil" where "prac-
tically nothing would grow ... except tumble-weed and flower-
ing sage." Even the sisters' garden after much toil produces
"very few vegetables" (p. 141). Their small farm seems to
belong, instead, in the drought-plagued terrain of To A God
Unknown. Thus, the central irony in The Pastures of Heaven,
that of the bountiful valley which promises a harvest of joy
and prosperity, but yields only disillusionment and pain, is

lost in this tale. The Lopez sisters merely pull up roots
from the rocky, starved soil and head north to San Francisco where their prospects seem brighter.

How might Steinbeck have concluded this tale had he
written it as an autonomous short story? Howard Levant
suggests that designing an adequate conclusion would not be
easy. The ending, he contends, would have to deal with
the tale's odd "juxtaposition of commercial and human systems
of value." "The Lopez sisters view themselves as perfectly honest women in a business world," says Levant, doing
nothing immoral in offering their sexual favors to customers
who buy at least three enchiladas.[22] Of course, the reader
knows that the "people of the valley" look upon these two
women much differently: "The whisper went about that the
Lopez sisters were bad women" (p. 149). Obviously, Rosa
and Maria deceive themselves. They believe that trading
sexual favors for the sale of enchiladas is somehow different
from selling their bodies directly. They refuse to see themselves the way their customers do--as prostitutes.

Some critics say that the Munroes act as destroyers of
the Lopez sisters' happiness. This position seems defensible
since Steinbeck inverts traditional morality, so that prostitution is made to look legitimate and respectable, while the
forces that try to crush it seem insensitive and inhumane.
Rosa and Maria do grow happier through their short-lived
commercial success: "Life became very pleasant ... the house
was filled with laughter and with squeals of enthusiasm" (p.
146). Given Steinbeck's tone of innocent humor about Rosa
and Maria's commercial venture, they are presented as another example of what Robert E. Morsberger calls Steinbeck's
"Happy Hookers." Typically, says Morsberger, Steinbeck
treats "the oldest profession with amused tolerance if not
downright sentimentality."[23]

Thus, Rosa and Maria become stereotypes, rather than
unique characters. Steinbeck gives us few details about
them, aside from their plumpness and soft hearts. Although
the women remain faceless, he mocks their religion, which
seems to offer them excuses for their unconventional behavior, rather than the inspiration and faith to change. As a
further slight to Rosa and Maria, their mule, Lindo, is far
and away the most lovingly described character in the story.
He stares with "heavy, philosophic sadness" and lifts "his

lips from his long, yellow teeth, and grins despairingly"
(p. 122). The mule seems to upstage its benefactors.   While
Lindo lends the story a light, humorous quality, considering
its barren landscape (inconsistent thematically with other
Pastures stories) and its contrived conclusion, the Lopez
sisters tale is one of the less successful pieces in the book.

"Molly Morgan"
(Ch. VIII)

Mimi Gladstein has observed that Steinbeck portrays
two kinds of women in his fiction: homemakers and whores.[24]
As a broad generalization this statement may be true, but
upon closer inspection of Steinbeck's characters, women in
other roles do emerge; and prominent among them are professionals of another stripe: school teachers.   Unlike the
housewives whom Steinbeck usually relegates to minor roles,
and the prostitutes whom he sometimes treats as window
dressing, school teachers are one group of women Steinbeck
takes seriously.   In his fiction they frequently become candidates for marriage to the community's most eligible men, and
always they are esteemed professionals, deeply respected and
admired.   Olive Hamilton (Steinbeck's own mother) in East of
Eden (1952) and Elizabeth Wayne in To A God Unknown
(1933) provide examples of this.   Perhaps the most fully
drawn character among them is the young school teacher in
The Pastures of Heaven, Molly Morgan.

Molly arrives in the Pastures to interview for a teaching position with the clerk of the school board, John Whiteside.   During this meeting, Molly describes the sunny side of
her life to Whiteside, while recalling only to herself (and the
reader) the darker side.   Her father had been a periodic
drunk who neglected his wife and three children.   Whenever
he returned from one of his frequent "business" trips, he
thrilled his children with tales of adventure in faraway
places.   Then one day he left and never returned.   After
two years, everyone except Molly gave him up for dead.
John Whiteside, hearing a carefully censored version of her
story, hires Molly and shelters her in his home, where
school board meetings are held.   At one board meeting Bert
Munroe jokes about his new drunken farm hand who boasts
of exotic travels.   Thinking of her father, Molly feels sick
and excuses herself from the meeting.   At the next board

gathering, Munroe again brings up the subject of the tipsy
farm hand, and Molly rushes away. Rather than risk dis-
covering the truth about her father, Molly resigns and leaves
the Pastures.

Steinbeck portrays Molly as a shy, unsure woman who
is easily intimidated by the careless remarks of Bert Munroe.
Yet in earlier chapters, Molly proves to be a more command-
ing figure. In the Tularecito tale (Ch. IV), Molly is the
"very young and very pretty" new teacher who makes "school
an exciting place where unusual things happened" (pp. 65-
66). She proves to be enthusiastic and intelligent, as well
as understanding. To this list of traits must be added sensitivity and sophistication, characteristics Molly Morgan uti-
lizes in her mediatory role between the people of the valley
(specifically the Munroes) and the non-conformist, Junius
Maltby (Ch. VI). She is also devoted to creativity and self-
expression. In a letter she writes: "'After the bare requi-
sites to living and reproducing, man wants most to leave
some record of himself, a proof, perhaps, that he has really
existed. He leaves his proof on wood, on stone or on the
lives of other people'" (p. 69). This creed of self-expression
is perhaps what motivates Miss Morgan to press Tularecito
into his ill-fated nocturnal search for gnomes. She wants to
leave her mark--"'some record of [her]self'"--on the life of
Tularecito.

All this adds up to a strangely different picture of
the young teacher than the one Steinbeck presents in Molly
Morgan's own story (Ch. VIII). Steinbeck shows us her
weaker, less admirable side. He foreshadows her ultimate
retreat from the valley through a series of five linked flashbacks which reveal Molly's past life.[25] The occasion for
these reminiscences is Miss Morgan's interview with John
Whiteside. Each censored statement she gives Whiteside is
followed by a long, revealing anecdote, known only to Molly
and the reader. The first illustrates young Molly's relationship with her affection-starved mother. The next introduces
Molly's salesman father, George Morgan, who returns home
"about once in every six months" (p. 167) bringing surprises,
gifts, and stories of adventure. In the third flashback,
Molly's father gives her a "dumpy, wooly puppy in a box"
(p. 170) which she names George, after him. The fourth
anecdote shows Molly's father stumbling home after one of
his periodic drunks. When Morgan disappears, the children

are forced to work; Molly enrolls in the Teacher's College at
San Jose, which is the subject of the fifth and final flashback.

These five intricately linked reminiscences, providing
a nearly complete story within the main tale, contribute to
the complexity of Steinbeck's well-crafted plot. In addition,
one brief interlude occurs, in which Steinbeck depicts Molly's
hike to the abandoned hut of the legendary hero and thief,
Vasquez. This solitary trek to the mountain hideout demonstrates Molly's tendency to romanticize such shadowy figures
as Vasquez and her negligent father. Steinbeck seems to
draw an analogy between the two men. Both are romantic
adventurers, but irresponsible or immoral. Bill Whiteside,
John Whiteside's son, calls Vasquez a thief and murderer,
and tells Molly her father is an "'irresponsible cuss.'" Per-
ceiving Molly's fragile hopes that her father is alive, Bill
replies, "'If he's alive, it's funny he never wrote'" (p. 179).
Thus Bill Whiteside is the kind of person Molly must avoid if
she is to retain her illusions about her father. And avoid
the young farmer she does, yet a more formidable spoiler
awaits--Bert Munroe.

Richard F. Peterson characterizes Molly's behavior as
an allegiance to the past, in that she protects "her childhood
memory of her father as a modern Galahad, even at the cost
of losing a pleasant home and a rewarding teaching position."[26] The story's conclusion, with Molly's exodus prompted
by Bert Munroe, is not entirely based upon the logic of the
materials in the story itself. Given what we've seen above,
Bill Whiteside would have been a more likely candidate than
Bert Munroe to destroy Molly's illusions.

"Raymond Banks"
(Ch. IX)

A robust, jolly man, Raymond Banks runs a chicken
farm which is a model of cleanliness and order. But one
thing about Banks puzzles, even horrifies, some Pastures
residents: his occasional visits to San Quentin to witness
executions. Bert Munroe, on a whim, asks Banks if he can
accompany him to a hanging. Banks acquiesces, saying he
must first write for permission to his friend, the warden of
San Quentin. Munroe is astonished at himself for making

such a request, and feels nauseated at the thought of a
hanging. Later when Banks receives approval from the warden to bring along his neighbor, Munroe backs out. He
tells a morbid story to Banks about an old man who hacks a
red rooster to a clumsy, bloody death. Munroe says he
fears that the execution will be just as grisly. Banks can-
cels his trip to San Quentin in disgust and for days grum-
bles about how Munroe soured his plans.

Raymond Banks' desire to witness hangings reflects
his need to experience profound, or as Steinbeck calls it,
"holy" emotion. Viewing the hanging itself is not what ex-
cites Banks: "Had he been alone in the death chamber with
no one present except the prisoner and the executioner, he
would have been unaffected" (p. 198). For Banks, catharsis
occurs only in the presence of others. He requires the company of his warden friend, reporters, and other witnesses
to help him experience the profound reality of death.

Although Banks may lack empathy, he does not relish
violence. That he detests needless bloodletting is obvious
from the care with which he quickly executes his chickens
to avoid their suffering. Moreover, Banks is visibly shaken
when Bert Munroe narrates to him the gruesome butchering
of a Rhode Island Red rooster. Banks never contemplates
the death of a chicken or a man with curiosity or cruelty.
The only kind of execution he condones is the efficient kind,
where prolonged misery for the victim is unthinkable. Thus,
one irony of the story involves Bert Munroe's ridiculing Banks
for observing hangings, while actually Munroe himself is the
more morbid.

Besides this irony, the Banks tale represents a step
toward Steinbeck's more sophisticated use of imagery and
symbol. Banks' farm buildings, white-washed "immaculate
and new" (p. 190) and his chickens "clean" and white, and
ducks "magnificent white" suggest purity and goodness. The
white of Banks' farm buildings and fowl is complemented by
the "dark" green square of alfalfa and kale that comprise his
acreage, signifying fertility, growth, and abundance. The
white chickens and ducks roaming contentedly on the expanse
of green are occasionally threatened by a "red-tail hawk" (p.
191). With this color imagery Steinbeck suggests that the
Banks' chicken farm is a good, clean place; its fields are
fertile, but not without dangers or evils. Steinbeck also

implies an animal quality about Raymond Banks by making
him "beef-red" in color.   Bank's nose and ears are "painfully burned and chapped" (p. 192) from the sun and his eyes
are "black as soot" (p. 192).   Yet the pervasive white of the
Banks' farm suggests that regardless of his questionable
trips to San Quentin, Banks is not a bad or immoral man.

Another feature of the story which indicates Steinbeck's
continued growth as a story writer is its carefully designed
plot.   While the ending, like most others in the volume, may
seem slightly contrived, it is not blatantly pasted on.   Steinbeck adequately foreshadows the conclusion with three appearances by Bert Munroe spaced at equal intervals.   Thus Bert's
change of heart about witnessing a hanging is not a complete
surprise to the reader.   Ultimately, Steinbeck reveals that
Bert's true character is just as it appears at his first meeting with Banks; Munroe simply lacks the strong stomach to
follow through on his morbid intentions.   Steinbeck does not
seem to condone the obtuseness of Raymond Banks either.
His casual attitude toward the execution of a fellow human
being does indicate an almost animal-like numbness.   Yet he
acts as innocently about it as would an animal, while Bert
Munroe seems to relish contemplating the gruesome details
of violent death.

"Pat Humbert"
(Ch. X)

When his parents die leaving him their farm, Pat Humbert is a lonely man of thirty-five.   In the farmhouse, a
stuffy parlor and sitting room seem to be haunted by his
deceased forebears.   Pat closes off the rooms and sleeps in
the barn but the two rooms continue to haunt him.   He neglects the house until it becomes engulfed by a huge mound
of roses.   One day Mae Munroe tells her mother she would
like to see the inside of Humbert's place, since it reminds
her of a Vermont home.   Pat overhears her and decides to
redecorate the old dwelling, Vermont style.   With a crowbar
he breaks into the closed-off rooms and destroys their contents.   Pat orders new furnishings and plans to invite Mae
Munroe over once the redecoration is completed.   When that
day comes, Pat learns that Mae is engaged to Bill Whiteside.
His dreams shattered, he trudges back to the barn and beds
down in the hayloft.

In the Pat Humbert story Steinbeck further explores
the narrative technique of using one dominant symbol as a
structural underpinning of the narrative. Accordingly, he
transforms the isolated Humbert farmhouse into a reflection
of its reclusive inhabitants. Sometimes the farmhouse seems
to embody the ghosts of Pat's deceased parents; their voices
continue to haunt him even after they are ten years in the
grave. Thus, the sitting room and especially the (funeral)
parlor of the house become synonymous with Mr. and Mrs.
Humbert. But the boarded, musty house also represents
Pat Humbert; the haphazard mode of decorating suggests
Pat's present life. Since his parents had imposed countless
restrictions on him, Pat was unable to initiate his own ideas
and plans even when they died. He "didn't know what to do
now that there was no one to demand anything of him" (p.
219). Work in the fields during the day helps him to forget
his loneliness, but each evening it again confronts him.
Even after he tries to alleviate his loneliness by mingling
with the people of the valley, Pat still fears the sitting room
and parlor, and never enters them.

Pat remains lonely because at the core of his being he
has no identity apart from his former role as subservient son
and errand boy. As long as he refuses to confront the sitting room and parlor, his loneliness persists. Pat becomes
exuberantly happy only after he crowbars open the door into
these two most feared rooms and, "brushing the cobwebs
from his eyes" (p. 235), literally destroys all the furnishings. This violent act is equivalent to Pat ridding his haunted mind of parents. He knocks out a partition and makes
the two small rooms--signifying his two parents--into one
larger room--the new Pat. His vitality grows as the fresh,
new interior becomes a reality. Yet with the ironic conclusion of the story, Steinbeck suggests that Pat's new initia-
tive comes to nought. Once he learns that Mae Munroe is
to be married to Bill Whiteside, Pat regresses to his former
state--fearing the farmhouse and believing that his parents'
ghosts still inhabit it.

The Pat Humbert story is compact and tightly organized, in contrast to the loose, episodic style of "Junius
Maltby" and "Tularecito." Pat Humbert is always before the
reader's eye. Steinbeck seems to turn the story into a
psychological case study of Pat--with other characters brought
in to mark his development. Hence there are no renegade

episodes; every scene has a causal relationship to what
comes before and after it. The narrative also contains
carefully-wrought imagery, reinforcing the mood of the various scenes. After Mr. and Mrs. Humbert's funeral, for example, "A piece of old brown newspaper scudded along the
ground and clung about Pat's ankles. He stopped and picked
it off, looked at it for a moment and then threw it away" (p.
220). This passage suggests Pat's desolation as a result of
his parents' deaths. We sense Pat reaching for an answer
in the "old brown newspaper," yet when it tells him nothing
he lets the wind carry it away. He seems somehow even
more alone after this small disappointment.

"The Whitesides"
(Ch. XI)

The longest and most complex story in The Pastures
of Heaven has as its subject the dream of Richard Whiteside
to build a dynasty in the peaceful California valley. Whiteside journeys alone to California in 1850 to escape a family
curse. In each of the last three generations, the Whitesides
have produced only one male heir. During the third generation (when Richard was born) their New England home burned
to the ground. Richard decides to found a new dynasty by
building a durable home in the Pastures of Heaven. Then,
ironically, history repeats itself. Richard marries Alicia,
who bears him one child, John. John attends Harvard, the
family alma mater, and then marries Willa, who gives birth
to one son, Bill. Bill breaks with tradition by moving to
Monterey at the insistence of his fiancee, Mae Munroe. Soon
after, Bert and Jimmie Munroe convince John Whiteside to
burn off some brush in his fields. When a spark is caught
up in a whirlwind, the Whiteside homestead catches fire, destroying the most important symbol of their heritage. Thus,
the curse has returned: after only one male heir is born in
each of three generations, the Whiteside family home goes up
in flames.

Although near the end of the tale Steinbeck attempts
to make the Munroes seem culpable for the Whitesides' un-
doing, neither Bert nor Mae nor Jimmie Munroe is truly to
blame. Since Richard Whiteside carries with him from New
England his own family curse, the logic of the story requires
that the new Whiteside "dynasty," like the old one, collapse

under its own weight. Long before Mae Munroe convinces
Bill Whiteside to begin their married life in Monterey--rather
than in the Whiteside homestead--Bill has tacitly rejected his
family heritage of the gentleman farmer. Bill's boyhood fail-
ure to listen to his father reading Herodotus, Thucydides,
and Xenophon signals this rejection.[27] Soon Bill begins to
view the Whiteside farm strictly as a business. When John
Whiteside gives his son a heifer, Bill immediately trades it
for a litter of pigs, which he in turn sells at a profit. This
speculating side of Bill emerges early in his life and foreshadows his eventual abandonment of the Whiteside agrarian
ideal, so that he may buy into a partnership in a Monterey
Ford agency.[28]

   Despite Bill's forsaking the Whiteside heritage, Steinbeck symbolically links the Whiteside family to their home.
Hawthorne's House of the Seven Gables (1851) and Poe's
"The Fall of the House of Usher" (1839) provide examples of
literary works in which a similar identification between family and home occurs. Yet since Steinbeck refers to the house
as symbol in several different ways, he tends to diminish its
impact. First, its white color is obviously a sign of the Whiteside dynasty. Second, its durable "eastern slate roof" (p.
251) signifies the Whitesides' steadiness and deep roots.
Third, their sitting room containing gilded volumes of the
ancients represents the family's Harvard tradition. Steinbeck spotlights the sitting room when one wall falls away
during the fire, opening the room to John Whiteside's full
view. He watches helplessly as flames lick up the arms of
his favorite leather chairs. A fourth symbol is the Whitesides' "Great Meerschaum Pipe." When first given to Richard
Whiteside by his father-in-law, the pipe is creamy-white in
color. Through time and use it turns to rich brown and
then to "black in which there were red lights" (p. 268).
This change seems to foreshadow the fire which destroys
the Whiteside home.

   None of these four symbols--the white house, the eastern slate roof, the sitting room, or the Meerschaum pipe--
convincingly takes precedence as the symbol of the Whiteside
tradition. Although flawed by this blurring of symbols, the
Whiteside saga is perhaps the most promising story in the
collection. Its symmetry of design is precise, since the
Whiteside family history repeats itself exactly. And Steinbeck underscores the irony of Richard Whiteside's plans to

build a dynasty by foreshadowing the doom to come. The
burning of the Whiteside home is no accident; we are prepared for it from the very beginning of the tale. What is
accidental, both thematically and structurally, is the en-
croachment of the Munroes. The Whiteside curse requires
no outside meddling to fulfill its ends. These imperfections
do not abrogate, however, Steinbeck's several artistic re-
finements in The Pastures of Heaven: rounder, more believable characters, plots that are frequently unified and
structurally sound, and, for the most part, carefully conceived symbols which imbue the tales with rich meaning.
Perhaps most important of all considering his later development as a story writer and novelist, Steinbeck rediscovers
the California region he knows and depicts best. These
numerous improvements set the stage for Steinbeck's best-
known short fiction from The Long Valley, to be examined
next.

Chapter Three

THE LONG VALLEY (1938) AND OTHER
SHORT FICTION OF THE 1930s

Introduction

Even before The Pastures of Heaven came off the press
in the autumn of 1932, Steinbeck had begun writing the first
of fifteen stories collected in The Long Valley (1938).[1] By
1934--his most prolific year in short fiction--he had composed
a total of thirteen tales destined for that volume. By 1936,
the two remaining pieces were completed. Before their publication in The Long Valley, however, most of these stories
appeared in newspapers and magazines--sometimes not until
three or four years after Steinbeck composed them. "The
Harness," for example, was written in summer, 1934, but not
published until June, 1938. Similarly, "The Chrysanthemums,"
composed in February, 1934, did not appear until October,
1937. This phenomenon, widespread among Steinbeck's Long
Valley stories, is illustrated in Table 1.

Until now the composition dates of several Long Valley
stories have been unknown. Thus formerly it was not possible to determine the exact sequence in which Steinbeck
wrote all fifteen selections, in order to gauge his development as a story writer. Table 1 allows us for the first time
to accomplish this; it also helps us to answer questions
critics have raised about the milieu of these stories.

Joseph Fontenrose, for example, expresses concern
that Steinbeck--"the socially conscious novelist" of the late
1930s--seldom alludes to "the depression and its problems"
in The Long Valley.[2] Table 1 suggests why these problems
rarely emerge in the stories: Steinbeck wrote all but two of
them early in the decade, before his full attention had been

TABLE 1:   THE LONG VALLEY STORIES:
Dates of Composition and First Publication

Story	Composed[a]	First Published[d]
"Saint Katy the Virgin"	before May 1932	Dec. 1936
"The Gift"	ca. June 1933	Nov. 1933
"The Great Mountains"	ca. Summer 1933	Dec. 1933
"The Murder"	ca. Fall 1933[b]	April 1934
"The Chrysanthemums"	February 1934	Oct. 1937
"The Promise"	Summer 1934[c]	Aug. 1937
"The Leader of the People"	Summer 1934	Aug. 1936
"The Raid"	Summer 1934	Oct. 1934
"The Harness"	Summer 1934	June 1938
"The White Quail"	Summer 1934	March 1935
"Flight"	Summer 1934	1938 in TLV
"Johnny Bear"	Summer 1934	Sept. 1937
"The Vigilante"	Summer 1934	Oct. 1936
"The Snake"	ca. 1935	June 1935
"Breakfast"	ca. 1936	Nov. 1936

a.   The dates and sequences of composition for most stories were verified through Steinbeck's published letters and his manuscript copybook in which nine of the Long Valley stories were written. However, some of the dates of composition, as indicated in Table 1, are estimates.   For a description of the copybook and its contents see Martha Heasley Cox, "The Steinbeck Collection in the Steinbeck Research Center, San Jose State University," Steinbeck Quarterly 11 (Summer-Fall 1978), 96-99.

b.   Although Thomas Kiernan says that Steinbeck wrote "The Murder" in Fall, 1933 (p. 186), considerable evidence suggests that he first composed it earlier, probably intending to include it in Pastures of Heaven (1932).   See Roy S. Simmonds, "Steinbeck's 'The Murder' A Critical and Bibliographical Study," SQ 9 (Spring, 1976), 45-57.

c.   Stories composed in Summer, 1934 appear in Table 1 in the order Steinbeck lists them on one copybook page entitled, "Record of stories completed summer of 1934."   "Flight," however, actually appears in the copybook before "The White Quail," and then "The White Quail" is followed by "Addenda to Flight," an epilogue not included in The Long Valley.

d.   The periodicals in which these stories were first published are listed in the bibliography.

turned to the Great Depression and its effects on California's
agricultural valleys. Thus, only faint whisperings of troubled times can be detected. And while Steinbeck does deal
directly with victims of the depression in the piece he composed last, "Breakfast," this sketch is the exception rather
than the rule. In other stories, such as "The White Quail"
and "The Raid," he merely hints at the impending malaise.
Because of this, some critics expecting more political awareness from Steinbeck called The Long Valley ideologically aim-
less and inconclusive. As Eda Lou Walton in the Nation puts
it: "These stories are clever, but they move toward nothing.... Nothing in the work seems resolved or progressing
toward resolution."[3]

The Long Valley's title has also raised eyebrows, since
it somewhat misleadingly suggests that all stories are set--as
in The Pastures of Heaven--in a single geographic area. Although this lends the collection an aura of unity, actually
few of the tales take place in the Salinas "long" Valley.
Lewis Owens argues that probably only "The Chrysanthemums," "The White Quail," "The Harness," and "Johnny
Bear" can be definitely linked to this valley.[4] "Saint Katy
the Virgin" transpires in a markedly different time and
place from that of the other stories in the volume. "Flight"
occurs "on the wild coast" just north of Big Sur; "The
Snake" is set on Cannery Row in Monterey; and "The Murder" takes place in the Santa Lucia range near "a tremendous stone castle," which in real life towers above the Corral de Tierra (i.e. The Pastures of Heaven).[5] Nearby in
these same mountains Steinbeck sets The Red Pony tales.
"Breakfast," later revised for inclusion in The Grapes of
Wrath (1939), probably shares the novel's San Joaquin or
Sacramento Valley backdrop. Finally, as Owens points out,
the settings in "The Raid" and "The Vigilante" are "inde-
terminant."[6]

Why does such an obvious discrepancy exist between
the selection of stories and the title of the volume? This
question can be at least partially answered by reviewing the
conditions under which The Long Valley was published.
Steinbeck, as Table 1 illustrates, had trouble selling his
stories of the early 1930s. However, when the successes of
Tortilla Flat (1935), In Dubious Battle (1936), and Of Mice
and Men (1937) increased his fame, most of his unpublished
stories of this decade were quickly snatched up by the

nation's top magazines.[7] Steinbeck finally had captured the
public's attention, and his current publisher, Covici-Friede,
intended to capitalize on his growing renown. Thus, by
1938 the climate seemed right to issue a volume of his collected stories. Although Steinbeck did not know it then,
Covici-Friede was experiencing "financial difficulties" and,
hence, they "needed another Steinbeck best-seller fast."
Therefore, Pat Covici "pressed" the young author for the
collection.[8]

In a letter to Elizabeth Otis (May 2, 1938) Steinbeck
expresses some surprise that his stories were to appear in a
collected edition so quickly: "I didn't know that Pat was
considering doing the short stories soon."[9] The Long Valley
was published in September, 1938, but even if it had enjoyed
immediate popularity, the book's sales probably would not
have saved Covici-Friede which declared bankruptcy later
that summer.[10]

The haste with which The Long Valley was rushed to
press may account for some of its organizational flaws. In-
dications are that the collection might have been improved
had Steinbeck given more time to selecting, revising, and
arranging the stories. On the other hand, it can be argued
that short of deleting such inappropriate tales as "Saint Katy
the Virgin," Steinbeck could have done little to enhance the
volume. He included every complete story he had written
during the 1930s, except "How Edith McGillcuddy Met R.L.S."
and "Case History," both composed in summer, 1934. The
former tale he had tried to publish earlier, but for reasons
discussed below, he decided to withdraw it. The latter,
which is actually more a philosophical disquisition than a
story, was unsuitable for the collection. Therefore, Steinbeck had little choice but to include every publishable story
of the decade, disparate though they were. Some observations about style and technique can be made, however, which
apply to nearly all selections in The Long Valley:

1. Plot and Symbol

Sometimes during his career as a story writer Steinbeck
found it difficult to create unified, organic plots. Occasionally he placed characters in forced situations or he contrived
action--particularly at the end of a story--to emphasize a

preconceived symbol or theme. This fault crops up in The
Pastures of Heaven, as we have seen, and also at times
in The Long Valley. Peter Lisca calls the conclusion of
"Flight" "theatrical," for instance, "because of its too perfect symbolic congruity."[11] And in "The White Quail" and
"The Harness," the import of each story's central symbol
seems too obvious. The effect of this, according to Brian
Barbour, is a mechanical structure with symbolic meanings
so fixed as to approach the condition of allegory.[12] Steinbeck's plotting in such stories as "The Gift" and "The Chrysanthemums," on the other hand, is superb. No tricks.
No contrivances. Every element in these tales is smoothly
connected and believable. Once Steinbeck learned to make
his stories perfectly coherent in this way, he was capable
of creating masterpieces.

2. Characterization

       Steinbeck's method of characterization in The Long
Valley has occasioned considerable debate. Edmund Wilson
calls his characters "rudimentary," conceived and presented
in animal, rather than human terms.[13] And Stanley Young
argues that Steinbeck's protagonists simply "struggle with
one primitive emotion after another." But in the same breath,
Young praises Steinbeck's sensitivity and sympathy for human
beings "on all levels of experience."[14] Indeed, several
characters emerging from these tales are unforgettable.
Joseph Warren Beach calls Elisa Allen in "The Chrysanthemums" "delicious," saying, "She is much less simple than
she seems."[15]

       Women characters, in general, play a more prominent
role in Steinbeck's short stories than they do in his novels.
In recent studies of Steinbeck's female characters, a dispro-
portionately large number of the women discussed have come
from the short fiction.[16] These characters (as discussed
above in reference to "Molly Morgan") are typically of two
kinds: housewives and hookers. Most of the latter group
turn up in the novels, while the short stories are usually
peopled with the former. Male characters include cattle
ranchers, farmers, blue-collar workers, nostalgic and lonely
old men, and boys journeying through the sometimes elusive
and difficult passage to "manhood."

3. Style, Imagery, and Point of View

Spare, crisp, and economical are the adjectives cus-
tomarily used to describe Steinbeck's prose in The Long Valley. A master of the objective style, he often renders details with picture-like accuracy. While his prose is lean, it
is also poetic. Images of color, light and darkness, plants,
and animals abound, and seem at times so vivid as to tell
the story themselves. Steinbeck's narrative point of view in
The Long Valley stories is generally third person. In tales
such as "Flight," Steinbeck remains outside the mind of his
protagonists. However, in "The White Quail" and others he
does venture into the central character's thoughts. Two exceptions to Steinbeck's usual third-person point of view are
"Breakfast" and "Johnny Bear," both first-person narratives.
After having difficulty with the first-person technique earlier
in his career (see "Adventures in Arcademy"), Steinbeck in
The Long Valley handles it more successfully.

4. Generic Variety

In his Long Valley stories, Steinbeck displays a wide
variety of generic forms, including stories of initiation,
sketches, parables, and even one beast fable. Though Brian
Barbour argues that this variety is not "the product of ex-
perimentation" and therefore "reveals confusion of purpose,"[17]
Steinbeck, on the contrary, enjoyed trying new forms. Once
he was able to achieve his artistic aims in a given form, however, he frequently moved on. Thus, Steinbeck seldom re-
peated himself, even though repetition was exactly what many
critics wanted from him. As Elmer Davis puts it, Steinbeck
followed his own impulses, "instead of letting the expectations
of his public push him into a groove."[18]

*   *   *

Over the years scholars and critics have traditionally
treated The Long Valley as if it comprised the entire canon
of Steinbeck's short fiction. As we have seen, this is not
the case. But although fewer than half of Steinbeck's stories are contained in the 1938 volume, it is easily accessible
(while the uncollected and unpublished pieces are not), and
is usually regarded as his finest performance as a writer of
short fiction.

"The Chrysanthemums"
(1937)

"The Chrysanthemums" is generally considered to be
one of Steinbeck's finest short stories. According to Roy S.
Simmonds, an early draft of the tale bears some likeness to
"The Harness," featuring a repressed husband and his shrew-
ish, frustrated wife.[19] That Henry Allen in the discarded
draft (like Peter Randall in "The Harness") intends to plant
many "acres of sweet peas" (p. 105) represents a striking
similarity between the two narratives.[20] But Steinbeck apparently had misgivings about his early version of "The
Chrysanthemums" and therefore rewrote the story. The
finished tale, as Simmonds explains, proved to be a masterpiece:

> It is remarkable that Steinbeck could, after all
> the problems he had been encountering, produce in
> what appears to have been one flowing surge of
> creativity the short story which Andre Gide com-
> pared favorably with the best of Chehkov and which
> Mordecai Marcus unequivocally regards as "one of
> the world's great short stories."[21]

"The Chrysanthemums" takes place at the Allen Ranch
in the foothills of the Salinas Valley. A December fog blan-
kets the fields as Elisa Allen, thirty-five, cuts down the old
year's chrysanthemum stalks in her garden. Her husband,
Henry, appears and suggests that they dine out that evening.
After Henry leaves, a covered wagon drawn by an old bay
horse and a burro pulls up to the house. The big, stubble-
bearded driver asks Elisa if she has any pots to mend. Although Elisa at first resists him, her initial reluctance melts
away when the tinker feigns interest in her garden. He
tells her that a lady on his route wants some chrysanthemum
seeds. Elisa excitedly gives him several sprouts in a red
pot. Then she finds two saucepans which the tinker repairs
for fifty cents. After the wagon pulls away, Elisa runs into
the house, bathes, and dresses for the evening. Henry returns and marvels at how "strong" she looks. As the two
are leaving for dinner in their roadster, Elisa sees the chrysanthemum sprouts lying in the road. The tinker has thrown
them away, keeping the red pot. She begins to weep, but
hides her tears from Henry.

Several critics have argued that it is the protagonist,
Elisa Allen who makes "The Chrysanthemums" a great short
story. Marilyn L. Mitchell, for example, calls Elisa one of
Steinbeck's "strong women"--a woman who has "a strength
of will usually identified" with men, as well as an "ambiguous combination of traditionally masculine and feminine
traits."[22] While these and other facets of Elisa's personality are no doubt responsible for much of the story's appeal,
ultimately Steinbeck's well-crafted plot and his skillful use
of symbol make the story great. As Brian Barbour puts it,
Steinbeck "succeeds in organizing this story in a way he
does nowhere else."[23] "The Chrysanthemums" is a product,
says Roy S. Simmonds, of "one flowing surge of creativity."[24]
That the author himself was more concerned with plot than
character when he wrote the story is evident in his February 25, 1934 letter to George Albee:

> I shall be interested to know what you think of
> the story, the Chrysanthemums. It is entirely dif-
> ferent [from "The Murder"] and is designed to
> strike without the reader's knowledge. I mean he
> reads it casually and after it is finished feels that
> something profound has happened to him although
> he does not know what nor how. It has had that
> effect on several people here.[25]

The element of surprise Steinbeck alludes to underlies
the difference in plot between "The Chrysanthemums" and his
other stories of the 1930s. The surprise hinges on these
few words: "Far ahead on the road Elisa saw a dark speck.
She knew" (p. 22). A small clump of chrysanthemum sprouts
tossed away by the tinker speaks silently but eloquently of
his opportunism and insincerity. Specifically, it betrays his
feigned interest in Elisa and her garden. In Aristotelian
terms, Elisa's discovery constitutes a "recognition scene," in
which she acquires vital knowledge previously withheld from
her. In addition, it brings about a "reversal," or change of
fortune, at least as far as her feelings are concerned. Elisa's
rejuvenated strength and womanhood are instantly destroyed
by the sight of her discarded chrysanthemum sprouts. The
effect is one Steinbeck had attempted in other stories, but
spoiled with contrived endings.

The magic of Elisa Allen's discovery is that it is

genuinely surprising, yet developed organically from materials
present in the story. It succeeds primarily because of Steinbeck's deft handling of the story's dominant symbol. Unlike
in "The White Quail," where Steinbeck directly equates a
bird with the protagonist, Mary Teller, or in "The Harness,"
where he identifies Peter Randall's shoulder brace and elastic
belt with Randall's nagging wife, in "The Chrysanthemums"
Steinbeck does not peg the dominant symbol to any single
idea or thing. In fact, the symbol's power increases during
the story precisely because of its ambiguity. Early in the
narrative, for example, the chrysanthemum stalks seem to
be phallic symbols, and Elisa's "over-eager" snipping of them
(p. 10) suggests castration. Then in the "rooting" bed (p.
12) Elisa herself becomes masculine, inserting the "little
crisp shoots" into open, receptive furrows. Later the sprouts
become Elisa's children,[26] when she explains lovingly to the
tinker how to care for them as if they were leaving home for
the first time (p. 17). As a dominant symbol, Elisa's chrysanthemums are the very backbone of the plot. Just as the
tinker's ability to use these plants in exploiting Elisa precipitates the rising action and climax of the story--when Elisa,
at the height of her emotion, reaches out for the tinker's
"greasy black trousers" (p. 18)--so too Elisa's recognition
that he has tossed her chrysanthemum sprouts into the road
brings about the catastrophe.

Although the story's greatness depends on this symbol
and Steinbeck's superbly-crafted plot, Elisa Allen, her husband, and the tinker cannot be overlooked. Of these three
characters, Henry Allen's role is the smallest. He utters
only a few lines, but these few are significant in measuring
changes in Elisa's feelings. The reader barely gets to know
Henry, not only because he speaks so little, but also because
Steinbeck neglects to describe him in any detail. Henry's
role is that of a regulator, or even a repressor, of Elisa's
behavior. At one point he tells her that she is "'playing
some kind of a game'" (p. 21). Then later he quips, "'Now
you're changed again'" (p. 23). Henry is somewhat frightened when Elisa boasts, "'I'm strong.... I never knew before how strong'" (p. 22). The established order he represents seems to be in jeopardy because of Elisa's boldness,
and consequently Henry almost loses his composure. But
when he looks "down toward the tractor shed," and then
brings "his eyes back to her, they [are] his own again.
'I'll get the car,'" (p. 22) says Henry. Then he commands,

"'You can put on your coat while I'm starting'" (italics
added). Henry again exerts his authority. Yet the fact
that Elisa purposely makes him wait while she dresses suggests that his authority does not go unquestioned.

The other male character, the itinerant pot mender,
lives for his own pleasure. As he tells Elisa, "'I ain't in
any hurry ma'am.... I aim to follow nice weather'" (p. 14).
With his large body, stubble-beard, and nomadic lifestyle,
he awakens Elisa's aboriginal energy (p. 13). She becomes
sexually excited ("Her breast swelled passionately.... Elisa's
voice grew husky" [p. 18]), and she reaches out to him with
"hesitant fingers." Much of their conversation has sexual
overtones, such as when Elisa says: "'Every pointed star
gets driven into your body'" (p. 18). This contrasts to
the bantering, formal dialogue between Elisa and her husband, Henry.

That the tinker has radically altered Elisa's behavior
is obvious from her excitement upon his departure. Her
shoulders "straight ... head thrown back," she runs into
the house, and with a burst of energy, tears "off
her soiled clothes," flinging "them into the corner" of her
room (p. 20). Normally a neat and tidy housekeeper, Elisa
now scatters her garments, caring little where they fall.
Given this change in her behavior, Elisa is, in Freudian
terms, an "ego figure"--attracted to the carefree tinker
(representing her "id" or primal self) but then checked
in this urge by her repressive husband (her "super ego"
or civilized self). In this way she resembles Peter Randall, the repressed protagonist in "The Harness."

Although we have already considered some aspects of
style, Steinbeck's point of view in this tale merits special
attention. It is third-person objective--the narrative remaining outside the minds of the characters. This narrative stance requires self-restraint by the author, and is
especially interesting since Steinbeck, nevertheless, is able
to impute various qualities to Elisa Allen without revealing
her inner-most thoughts. Much of the ambiguity--and the
appeal--of Elisa Allen comes from the reader's never knowing
precisely what she is thinking. (Compare Mary Teller in
"The White Quail," to whose ruminations the reader is privy.)
Elisa remains a mystery because she seldom thinks out loud,
and never reveals exactly what the chrysanthemums mean to

her. The objective style insures the ambiguity of Elisa's
character and helps to make "The Chrysanthemums" one of
Steinbeck's finest short stories.

"The White Quail"
(1935)

During 1934 when he was composing the bulk of his
Long Valley stories, Steinbeck recorded feelings of severe
loneliness despite his marriage of nearly five years. Although he rationalized that his desolation was making him
more productive than he might otherwise have been, that it
troubled him is suggested by the several lonely characters
in The Long Valley, especially Harry Teller in "The White
Quail."[27] Another personal concern of Steinbeck's at this
time was the fear of change. He "had experienced a profound sense of change in his life during the fatal illness of
his mother and the wasting away of his father." His relationship with his sister, Mary, and with his wife had also altered
sharply. After fighting his own perplexity over these changes, Steinbeck came to believe that "what was wrong with the
world was that so many people irrationally feared and resisted
the inevitability of change."[28]

Steinbeck's feelings about these two obstacles to human
happiness--loneliness and the fear of change--emerge through
the two characters in "The White Quail." Mary Teller is a
housewife whose garden is a model of perfection: lush
cinerarias, a heart-shaped pool, and a wall of beautiful
fuchsias. Mary had dreamt of this garden long before she
met the man who made it possible--her husband, Harry Teller. Harry hires workmen to landscape the garden to Mary's
specifications. She supervises them so closely that the garden emerges a floral reflection of herself--beautiful and
changeless. Fear of change is implicit in Mary's question to
her husband about the garden: "'We won't ever change it,
will we, Harry? If a bush dies, we'll put another one just
like it in the same place'" (p. 30). One afternoon when a
white quail alights among her flowers, Mary believes the
bird is the essence of herself. Suddenly a grey cat threatens the quail and Mary screams, scaring the feline away.
Harry comforts his wife, and promises to shoot (but not
kill) the cat early the next morning. After spending the
night alone (Mary sleeps by herself in her own bedroom),

Harry approaches the garden with his air rifle and shoots
not the cat, but the white quail. He mutters to himself that
he didn't mean to hurt the bird, but feels terribly alone.[29]

The biographical nature of "The White Quail" may explain what Stanley Young calls its "unusual emotional prov-
ince."[30] A reflection of Steinbeck's life during this time,
the narrative can be seen as a study of a failing marriage,
which focuses first on the wife's fixation and aloofness from
her husband, and then on the husband's consequent loneliness and resentment. Brian Barbour points out that such a
shift in focus (from Mary to Harry Teller) diminishes the
story's emotional power,[31] for what begins as an expose of
Mary's diseased imagination, culminates in a flash of violence
when Harry kills the symbol of his wife's changeless purity--
the white quail. The story ends without resolution. Harry,
as a result of shooting the quail, feels remorse and increased
loneliness. Mary remains unchanged.

Over the years, critics have suggested other themes
for "The White Quail." The most unusual among them is
Arthur L. Simpson's contention that Mary Teller constitutes
Steinbeck's "Portrait of an Artist" (i.e., she is obsessed
with her artistic creation [garden] to the exclusion of human
warmth and compassion).[32] Other critics have seen the
story as the chronicle of a narcissist, the tale of a Platonic
idealist, and a symbolic representation of sexual tension ex-
ploding into violence.[33] But the themes of loneliness and
fear of change are particularly central, since each can be
identified with one of the two characters, and both feelings
are evidenced in the life of the author at this time.

The story's setting, like Mary Teller's garden, is unusually static. The scene never shifts from the Teller home
and yard. The plot unfolds in six numbered sections, each
indicating a change in time. Between sections one (Harry's
proposal) and two (landscaping of the garden), the longest
stretch of time elapses. Except when a cat threatens the
white quail in section one and when Harry shoots the quail
in section six, the story has little overt action. In addition
to giving the story a generally static setting, Steinbeck
omits details about the physical appearance of the characters.
The reader may not notice this omission, though, since Mary's
psyche is so thoroughly linked with her garden, and her
"essence" with the white quail. Harry, on the other hand,

is identified with the "grey cat" (p. 39) preying on Mary's
quail. He not only refuses to poison the cat, but also kills
the symbolic bird. Antoni Gajewski equates Harry with such
other "enemies" as snails, dogs, and common garden pests
that plague Mary.[34]

The story's principal strength is neither in its plot
nor its characters. Its distinctive quality can more accu-
rately be called "lyric." Like a lyric poem, "The White
Quail" is primarily an expression of the writer's emotions--
loneliness and the fear of change, as we have seen. But,
below the level of the author's consciousness, more sinister
meanings surely lurk. The white quail represents beauty,
purity, and helplessness, and is the crowning glory of Mary's
private, ordered, and timeless garden. The cat is a predator, a threat to the symbol of Mary's inner self. Whether
Harry realizes it or not, he has an affinity with the cat.
And whether he wills it or not, he shoots quail, not cat.

"Flight"
(1938)

When discussing Steinbeck's "Flight" in 1972, John M.
Ditsky remarked that the story had "aroused surprising lit-
tle critical comment."[35] Today this statement no longer ap-
lies, since relative to all short stories in the Steinbeck canon,
"Flight" has been perhaps the most popular subject for criti-
cal articles. One recent bibliography shows that only "The
Chrysanthemums" and "The Leader of the People" rival
"Flight" for this distinction.[36]

Although "Flight" has provoked a flurry of criticism,
the narrative is spare and can be quickly summarized:
About fifteen miles south of Monterey, the Torres family
farm clings to a sloping acreage above the Pacific Ocean.
Nineteen-year-old Pepé, the oldest of three children, is
sent to town for medicine by his mother. He wears the black
hat and rides in the saddle of his deceased father. Once in
Monterey, Pepé drinks too much wine, gets into a fight, and
kills a man. Returning home, he saddles a fresh horse and
flees into the Santa Lucia Mountains. Pepé rides for several
days trying to outdistance the ominous "dark watchers" who
pursue him. Although at first prepared with food, water,
and a rifle, Pepé loses these, as well as his horse, on the

trail. Before long he is fatigued and helpless--an easy prey
for the bullets of the "dark watchers." Mortally wounded,
Pepé tumbles from a mountaintop and starts a small avalanche
which finally covers his head.

In his influential 1940 article, "The Californians: Storm
and Steinbeck," Edmund Wilson singles out "Flight" as an example of what he calls Steinbeck's tendency to assimilate "human beings to animals." The "young Mexican boy," says Wilson, "is finally reduced to a state so close to that of the
beasts that he is apparently mistaken by a mountain lion for
another four-footed animal."[37] Peter Lisca in The Wide World
of John Steinbeck (1958) expands Wilson's literal reading in
the story by demonstrating that "Flight" is a moral allegory
operating on two levels: first, the physical level, which involves Pepé's literal "separation from civilized man and his
reduction to the state of wild animal"; and second, the symbolic level (moving in the opposite direction), which shows
"how man, even when stripped of all his civilized accoutre-
ments ... is still something more than an animal." On the
symbolic level, Lisca contends that Pepé faces his doom "not
with the headlong retreat or futile death struggle of an animal, but with the calm and stoicism required by the highest
conception of manhood." By offering this broader interpretation of the story, Lisca opened the way for subsequent
readings which went on to discuss Pepé's journey as the
initiation of a child into the adult world.[38]

In the typical initiation story the protagonist grows and
changes until, through various rites of passage, he or she
reaches maturity. "Flight" is somewhat more complex and
ambiguous than this, however, since Pepé's initiation leads
to his death. Consequently, M.R. Satyanarayana likens
"Flight" to the Greek myth of Phaëthon, in which a son of
Helios, when permitted to drive the chariot of the sun, is
struck down with a thunderbolt by Zeus. Thus, in becoming a man, the boy dies.[39] This tragic twist in Pepé's initiation can be seen as simply another element in the story,
or as its governing principle. Viewing "Flight" according
to the latter criterion, Warren French identifies Pepé's swift
regression into a hunted animal as a naturalistic tragedy.[40]
Some confusion occurs, however, when we see Pepé as the
protagonist of both a naturalistic tragedy and an initiation
story. Brian Barbour, speaking of the instability caused
by such a combination, contends that "the elements work

against one another."[41] According to Barbour, Steinbeck's
marriage between these two forms is not a harmonious one.

   Although his flight ends in death, as the protagonist
of an initiation story Pepé is not one character, but two.
At the beginning of the narrative he is a boy; at the conclusion, a man. Yet the point at which he is transformed
from a boy to a man has been a matter of contention. Early
in the tale Pepé is referred to as a lazy "'peanut,'" a "'coyote,'"
and a "'foolish chicken,'" yet he returns from his overnight
journey to Monterey as a different person: "He was changed.
The fragile quality seemed to have gone from his chin" (p.
51). From this description, Pepé's arrival into manhood is
unequivocal. Yet some critics believe that the real test of
his manliness, and hence the real proof he is a man, comes
only at the story's end, when Pepé rises on a mountain top
to greet his death heroically.[42] One extreme view is that
Pepé never attains manhood, since he is unequipped mentally
to cope with the adult world.[43] Throughout the narrative,
however, Steinbeck takes pains to present Pepé in the best
possible light. For example, Steinbeck excludes the early
scene in Monterey when Pepé kills a man to "avoid showing
his protagonist acting senselessly, without thought, and
fatefully."[44] Pepé merely recalls the murder in summary
form (the incident fills only one paragraph) to Mama Torres,
so that the reader will understand the reason for his flight,
while not losing interest in or sympathy for the youngster.

   The Torres farm from which Pepé departs on his journey hangs precariously on a sloping cliff above the "hissing
white waters of the ocean." The harsh hand of nature can
be felt in the "rattling, rotting barn ... grey-bitten with sea
salt" (p. 45). A measure of pessimism imbues this landscape,
as if Steinbeck intended to suggest that environmental factors
govern the lives of the Torres family. And the dark, brooding coastal range into which Pepé flies is synonymous with
death itself. Lewis Owens says that along with Pepé, Joseph
Wayne in To a God Unknown (1933), Gitano in "The Great
Mountains" (1933), and several other Steinbeck characters
trek into these same mountains to die.[45] The moon, a stun-
ning white orb when Pepé departs, follows him up the slopes,
rising and descending during the several nights of his journey. Antoni Gajewski suggests that when the moon rises,
Pepé is vigorous and strong; when it descends, his strength
wanes. In addition, several animals suggest Pepé's condition

as he proceeds into the mountains. A wildcat (p. 60) and
eagle (p. 62) indicate power and perseverance. A rattlesnake and some lizards (p. 64) imply cunning and
weakness. And "little birds" (p. 65) looking upon him without fear and buzzards (p. 63) circling above in search of
carrion portend Pepé's doom. [46] At other times, animals
preying upon one another suggest by analogy the "dark
watchers" in their pursuit of Pepé. Doves and quail run
out to a spring, for example, but are soon encroached upon
by a "spotted wildcat" (p. 60). This incident becomes a parable of Pepé's flight--the birds suggesting Pepé, and the
wildcat, the dark watchers.

Steinbeck portrays this scene and others in the story
with a style that is spare and economical. Peter Lisca says
that this suggests a debt to Hemingway: "a crisp rendering
of factual details which, while staying close to the actual ob-
ject and action, avoids the myopic distortions of 'realistic'
writing." [47] As in other artistically successful stories like
"The Chrysanthemums" and "The Gift," Steinbeck's point of
view in "Flight" is third-person objective. The narrator remains outside the mind of his protagonist. Much of the mystery, ambiguity, and suspense in "Flight" stems from this
objective stance. Steinbeck emphasizes external events--
vivid physical action fills the story, and he refuses to trans-
late this action into a clear-cut message or moral.

"The Snake"
(1935)

"I wrote the story just as it happened.... I don't
know what it means." [48] With these words, Steinbeck explains that his enigmatic tale, "The Snake," recounts a real
incident which occurred in the laboratory of his biologist
friend, Ed Ricketts. As A. Grove Day, a friend of Steinbeck for many years, recalls the episode, once when he and
Steinbeck were in Ricketts' laboratory a woman dropped and
hurt a white mouse she had been playing with. Someone
suggested they feed the mouse to a rattlesnake Ricketts'
father had found on a golf course. All watched as a gro-
tesquely funny thing happened. Upon swallowing the whole
mouse except its tail, the snake with the thin protuberance
from its jaws looked as if it were smoking a cigarette. [49] In
the story, Steinbeck substantially changes this incident, as

Day remembers it. Ricketts, called "Dr. Phillips," arrives
one morning at his laboratory on the cannery street in Monterey carrying a sack of starfish. With their sperm and ova,
he begins a series of timed embryo experiments, when suddenly a tall, slim woman enters the laboratory. She waits
for him momentarily, and then asks if she may buy a male
rattlesnake. Once the purchase is arranged, she asks to
see her snake eat. Dr. Phillips reluctantly agrees, placing
a large white rat into the rattler's cage. As the snake
poises to strike, Dr. Phillips notices that the woman duplicates exactly its movements. Her bizarre behavior so un-
nerves him, that he forgets one sequence of his embryo experiment. Angrily, he pours the ruined contents into the
sink. Although the woman says she will return occasionally
to visit her snake, Dr. Phillips never sees her again.

"The Snake" is one of the few short stories in which
Steinbeck focuses on a single time, place, and action. The
time elapsed is less than an hour. The sole setting, a
laboratory, suggests the quasi-clinical conditions under which
animal (and human) behavior can be observed. The plot
focuses on one action. Events proceed chronologically, sometimes slowly, creating an aura of suspense. The incessant
washing of waves against the laboratory pilings counterpoints
and relieves the slow but steady progress of the narrative.
These waves also evoke a primitive atmosphere, in keeping
with the bizarre, primordial movements of the female visitor.
On one occasion, Dr. Phillips cannot distinguish between the
water's quiet splash among the piles and the woman's sigh.[50]

Since Steinbeck clearly had Ed Ricketts in mind when
he wrote "The Snake," the author's attitude toward his friend
becomes a key to understanding the fictional character, Dr.
Phillips. In "About Ed Ricketts," Steinbeck affectionately
calls Ricketts "half-Christ and half-goat," "an original," a
"complex and many-faceted" man who thought in "mystical
terms." Steinbeck tells us that Ricketts' tastes were catho-
lic, running from cold beer to Gregorian chants to women of
all types and dispositions.[51] In the story Dr. Phillips reacts
emotionally to the bizarre woman who disrupts his embryo experiment. According to Warren French, Steinbeck knows
that "one's attitude can be simultaneously scientific and emotional."[52] Thus, he characterizes Dr. Phillips as both a dis-
passionate observer of nature, as well as a sensitive, feeling
human being.

John Steinbeck, 1961.   (Courtesy of the Steinbeck Library,
Salinas, CA)

John, Thom, and John IV Steinbeck. See "His Father."
(Valley Guild, Courtesy of the Steinbeck Library, Salinas,
CA)

Corral de Tierra. See The Pastures of Heaven. (James
Speck, courtesy of the Steinbeck Library, Salinas, CA)

Here we are. Mary, John & Dick – Salinas Aug 26.07

Ed Ricketts, Dr. Phillips in "The Snake." (Courtesy of the Steinbeck Library, Salinas, CA)

[Opposite:] John and Mary Steinbeck on Jill, 1907. See The Red Pony and "The Summer Before." (Valley Guild, Courtesy of the Steinbeck Library, Salinas, CA)

"The Castle" in Corral de Tierra. See "The Murder."
(Maurice Dunbar)

[Opposite:] Castroville, CA. See "The Days of Long
Marsh" and "Johnny Bear." (Courtesy of the Steinbeck
Library, Salinas, CA)

Fisherman's Wharf near Cannery Row. See "The Snake."
(Vince Colletto, courtesy of the Steinbeck Library, Salinas,
CA)

Ed Ricketts' Lab on Cannery Row. See "The Snake."
(R. S. Hughes, Jr.)

The tall, slim woman who unexpectedly enters Dr.
Phillips laboratory brings his character into high relief. Unable to divert his feelings toward her, Dr. Phillips becomes
"piqued" (p. 77) because the woman shows no interest in his
embryo experiment. Consequently, he tries to "arouse" and
"shock" her by embalming a "limp dead cat" (p. 77), but she
merely makes him more "nervous" (p. 78). Then, when she
asks to buy a snake, he becomes "afraid" (p. 80) and later
angry. Her attempt to reach into the snake's cage leaves
Dr. Phillips "shaken" (p. 81) and a feeling of sorrow, and
again anger, arises in him when he puts the rodent into the
cage (p. 82). Finally, his emotions are wrought up to high
pitch when the rattler prepares to strike. "He felt the blood
drifting up in his body.... His veins were throbbing ..."
(p. 83). "'Perfect,'" he cries. "'[I]t was an emotional bath,
wasn't it?'" (p. 84). The woman does not respond, and Dr.
Phillips' anger boils again when he realizes that his embryo
experiment has been ruined (p. 85). Thus we witness the
wide amplitude of Dr. Phillips' feelings.

French suggests that the central focus of the story is
not so much the strange woman as it is "what she allows us
to learn about another."[53] "Another," of course, is Dr.
Phillips. But the woman herself is quite an enigmatic character, probably one of the most bizarre in Steinbeck's fiction. Charles E. May characterizes her as a Jungian anima
figure who has emerged from the primal, mythic world to jar
Dr. Phillips out of what May calls his "scientific and therefore detached existence." Dr. Phillips, according to May,
"has rejected the unconscious to such an extent that the
instinctual forces [the woman] rise up in opposition."[54]
This argument, although debatable as it pertains to the
biologist, marks a new approach to the puzzling woman, who
had formerly been discussed by critics only in Freudian and
biblical terms. Peter Lisca, for instance, contends that by
watching the male rattler eat the white rat, the woman "ob-
jectifies her [sexual] frustration."[55] And Joseph Fontenrose
calls her a fascinated creature in a "zoological garden of
Eden."[56]

Steinbeck was apparently so enamored with this woman
and her snake fixation that he recounted a variation of the
incident in chapters 16 and 17 of Sweet Thursday (1954).
In this latter rendition, the biologist's intruder, rather than
a snake-like woman, is Suzy, a new "girl" at the Bear Flag

Restaurant. This time what ruins the starfish embryo experiment is not a snake, but an argument between Suzy and the
doctor, which shows him to be a lonely man deluding himself
with dreams of writing what Suzy calls a "'great big goddam
highfalutin paper.'"[57] Doc, admirably, realizes a true thing
when he hears it, and begins to alleviate his loneliness by
falling for Suzy. Although much of the suspense of the original story is lost in this retelling of "The Snake," its inclusion in Sweet Thursday testifies to Steinbeck's enduring
pleasure in the tale.

"Breakfast"
(1936)

     Like the story, "The Snake," "Breakfast" is another
short work that Steinbeck incorporated into one of his novels.
A revised version of this piece appears in Chapter 22 of The
Grapes of Wrath (1939). But to call "Breakfast" a narrative
fragment is misleading, since it was published some three
years earlier than Steinbeck's famous novel. A more accurate
term is "sketch," a "brief composition simply constructed and
usually most unified in that it presents a single character, a
single incident. It lacks a developed plot or very great characterization."[58] On all counts, except perhaps for the arbi-
trary "single character," "Breakfast" fits this definition.[59]

     Steinbeck opens the sketch with a first-person narrator
walking along a country road before sunrise. Ahead in the
gathering light he sees a tent. Beside it a young woman,
nursing a baby, cooks bacon and biscuits. Two stubble-
bearded men in dungarees emerge from the tent, and the
older one invites the passerby to join them for breakfast.
He gladly accepts. The three men squat around a packing
case, while the woman sets out a tin platter. They eat
quickly. Afterwards, when the two male hosts stand and
face the eastern dawn, the rising sun reflects brilliant light
in the older man's eyes. They ask their guest to pick cotton with them that day, but he thanks them and walks off
alone down the road.

     Steinbeck's choosing an incident with an obvious be-
ginning, middle, and end gives this sketch unity. "Breakfast" is unusually symmetrical: it opens with one paragraph
addressed directly to the reader and closes in the same way.

In both paragraphs, the narrator tries (but admits he is unable) to explain why the incident is memorable. The sun's
journey from behind the eastern mountains across the sky
also adds to the symmetry of the sketch. Its westward progress from dawn to sunrise frames the morning communion
between the migrant family and the narrator. The faint illumination of the twilight brings the migrants' tent into the
narrator's view. The sky continues to redden, as the nursing mother prepares biscuits and bacon. Once the family
and guest sit down to share their repast, the sun climbs
above the mountaintop with a "reddish gleam" (p. 92). Finally, when the two bearded men face east, the sunlight reflects in the older man's eyes.

The auroral splendor of daybreak helps to account for
the warm "pleasure" (p. 89) and the "element of great beauty"
(p. 92) the narrator feels in recalling the scene. The sunrise is majestic. Its brilliant scarlet light piercing through
darkness lifts the narrator's spirits. The steaming hot biscuits, bacon, and coffee shared by the migrant family also
inspire him. The meal becomes a feast for the narrator's
senses. He is no doubt surprised at his hosts' generosity,
considering they possess few of life's material comforts. Although they have little, they give a lot. Their humble repast becomes a ritual of holy communion, suggesting an in-
domitable faith in the brotherhood of man.60

The first-person narrator's participation in the episode
brings the reader close to the action and provides a unity of
impression that is lost in the revised, third-person point of
view sketch included in The Grapes of Wrath. In this latter
rendition the austere beauty of the sunrise and the spiritual
significance of the shared meal lose much of their impact. In
addition, Steinbeck abandons his rigid principle of selection
which makes "Breakfast" a spare, crisply focused narrative:
he adds more dialogue--mainly small talk--and moves the migrants' lone tent from a quiet country road to a campground
filled with other tents. Thus the solitude and serenity of
the event is lost with the incursion of civilization. The atmosphere of the original lacking, the memorable sketch becomes
an easily forgotten scene in the novel.61

"The Raid"
(1934)

One of the few short stories in The Long Valley which
ostensibly deals with topical issues of the 1930s is "The
Raid." The story takes place one dark night in a California
town. Two men emerge from a lunch wagon, Dick asking
his younger companion, Root, if he has prepared his speech.
The frightened youth answers in the affirmative, but worries
about a possible raid. Walking toward the outskirts of town,
they reach a deserted store and begin to prepare for an eight
o'clock meeting. Root tacks up one poster portraying a man
in harsh reds and blacks and a second bearing a large red
symbol. Next he sets out a pile of leaflets and paper-bound
books. At half past eight when no one has arrived, Root's
fear intensifies. Then a man appears, warning that a raid-
ing party is on the way. Dick encourages Root to stand
firm. Suddenly a crowd of angry men rushes the building.
Root begins his speech, but is knocked down by a flying
two-by-four. The two men take a horrible beating. Sometime later, Dick and Root awaken bandaged in the hospital
cell of a jail. Dick congratulates the younger man for not
running under fire.

While "The Raid" concerns the plight of two communist
organizers, many critics have found that their political ideol-
ogy is less important than Steinbeck's psychological portrait
of the younger man's grappling with fear. Steinbeck focuses
on the novice party organizer, Root, and contrasts his behavior with that of a veteran, Dick. The essential difference
between these two characters becomes the crux of the story.
While both men are no doubt frightened by the raid, the
seasoned activist, Dick, has learned to mask his fears under
a facade of party slogans. The inexperienced Root, on the
other hand, openly expresses his trepidation. Yet, when a
swarm of angry vigilantes attack the two, Root proves himself. He stands alongside Dick, unflinching at flying fists
and debris. Thus, "The Raid" has been correctly called an
initiation story, for Root overcomes his dread and is initiated
into the brotherhood of veteran activists. The victory recorded in the story, therefore, is not of communism over
capitalism, or vice versa, but, in Antoni Gajewski's words,
a "victory of a human being over human nature."[62] Con-
troling his fear regardless of the danger present is the
lesson Root learns.

Dick and Root's stand against the vigilantes also has
religious overtones. Peter Lisca notices a parallel between
the two men and the martyrs of early Christianity. Even
though Dick and Root have been tipped off about the raid,
both men choose to face the onslaught with what amounts to
religious zeal for the "cause" and for the portrait of the
venerable man behind them. The human image on that poster becomes a god to the pair, and they are his disciples.
Root, says Lisca, resembles Christ, for he undergoes a ritual death at the hands of the angry mob and is then reborn
into a staunch, unwavering supporter of the party.[63] Dick,
as mentioned above, is a diehard party regular and already
knows how to stand firm.

This brings up the essential difference between these
two characters: while Dick is static, hardened into his
opinions and behavior by party dogma, Root is dynamic and
changes as the narrative progresses. Dick is Root's model
for emulation, but perhaps because the older man obeys party
orders unflinchingly, he is a somewhat less interesting character than Root. On the surface, Dick maintains a facade of
unbending resolve which contrasts vividly with Root's apparent wavering. That Dick is not impervious to his subordi-
nate's alarm, however, becomes evident when he warns Root:
"'Oh! Shut up, kid. You'll get my goat pretty soon'" (p.
100) and "'Keep still, will you? You'll drive me nuts'" (p.
101). But, otherwise, Dick is the hardboiled activist. Even
his peajacket suggests the tough, outer shell that such a
man must don. And for the most part, his speech is laconic
and curt, except when he elaborates on party doctrine.
Thus, instead of expressing his own feelings, he quotes
Marx. Dick's advice to Root betrays this fear of expressing
feelings: "'[D]on't go opening up for everybody to show them
how you feel'" (p. 102).

In this respect, Root is the exact opposite of Dick.
He cannot contain his fright, and lets it slip off his tongue
in unchecked profusion. At first, Root behaves like a "cry-
baby, a shrinking boy who lacks faith in his own strength."[64]
In fact, Root resembles a vulnerable infant from the beginning
of the story. Unlike Dick who wears a hard outer shell (the
peajacket), Root's apparel is a "blue turtle-neck sweater"
(p. 95), suggesting softness. When Dick first accuses him
of being scared, the young novice puts on his "toughest
look" (p. 95), implying that Root is unsure of his toughness.

And like a small boy, he speaks in a lonely, homesick voice
when Dick questions him about his father (p. 96). Once the
raid is imminent, Root finally admits, "'Yes, I'm scared. May-
be I won't be no good at this'" (p. 103). Thus, Steinbeck
clearly establishes that Root is untested.

Suspense, a key dramatic device in "The Raid," increases as a result of Steinbeck's consistent focus on Root's
fears. Root questions Dick: "'[Y]ou didn't hear nothing about
no raid, did you?'" (p. 98). Out of nervousness, the young
novice asks Dick on four separate occasions for the time.
Dick's grudging replies set up the chronology of the story.
Since the meeting is scheduled to begin at eight o'clock, each
minute that elapses after eight increases the organizer's an-
xiety. On the last occasion when Root asks for the time,
Dick replies: "'Quarter-past nine'" (p. 106). That the meeting participants are over an hour late signals danger.

Night sounds also add suspense. Rustling winds, barking dogs, and rumbling motor cars are heard outside the deserted store where Dick and Root prepare for the meeting.
Steinbeck repeats variations on this motif six times (pp. 98,
100, 101, 103, 104, and 105). In the culminating sequence,
he adds two new sounds, a train and an alarm clock (p. 105).
Some specific sounds: the wind rustling through the locust
trees and the murmuring of automobiles--the mutter of en-
gines (p. 100), the squeal of brakes (p. 104), and the sound
of horns (p. 100)--foreshadow the coming of the vigilantes.
Just before the raiders arrive, Steinbeck ingeniously height-
ens the suspense with complete silence (p. 105). The wind
rushes fiercely and then dies away. Dogs stop barking, the
thundering train disappears, the alarm clock falls silent.

"The Raid" is divided into four numbered sections which
mark the progress of Root's initiation. M.R. Satyanarayana
suggests that within these sections, Root goes through all
the well-known rites of passage except change of name.
These include: "(1) the hero's severance from the mother,
(2) the revelation of the mystery of adult experience, (3)
the ordeal, and (4) the symbolic death and rebirth."[65]
These sections form the infra-structure of the plot. The
point of view is third-person omniscient, for the narrator
imputes certain thoughts and feelings to Root which the
reader would not learn of otherwise. The narrator's om-
niscience is crucial in depicting the psychological portrait

of a young protagonist grappling with almost insurmountable
fears. Thus, Root's victory over his fright is the focus of
the story.

"The Harness"
(1938)

"The Harness" is a psychological study of Salinas Valley farmer and widower, Peter Randall. Upon the death of
his wife, Randall becomes hysterical. To his friend Ed Chappell's surprise, Randall sheds his clothes revealing a shoulder
harness and stomach belt—both of which he then removes.
(They were Emma's idea.) He also confides that his annual
"business trips" to San Francisco actually have been week-
long orgies (to get away from Emma). Now with his wife
gone, Randall vows to indulge himself daily, living without
restraint. As a symbol of his liberation, he plants forty-
five acres of sweet peas, a financially risky crop (Emma
would have disapproved) which luckily pays off. Later in a
San Francisco hotel, Ed Chappell encounters Randall returning on a drunken spree from the city's houses of prostitution.
Randall hasn't changed. For a while he has shed the physical symbols—the harness and stomach belt—of his wife's domination, but he confesses that she continues to rule his mind.

Peter Randall is fifty, grave, and blue eyed, with a
"carefully tended beard" (p. 111) and perfect posture. The
telling feature of his personality, however, is the chained
impulse within him, the "force held caged" (p. 111). In
Jungian terms, Randall fails to achieve oneness, since the
two sides of his personality remain at odds. The rejected,
darker side (his "shadow") wars with the exemplary, public
side (his "persona"). Thus, although Peter consciously ad-
vocates libidinous pleasures, the fact that he cannot inte-
grate such pleasures into his everyday life means that he
actually rejects them. When he runs off to San Francisco
to indulge his senses, Peter merely allows himself to be
"bad" temporarily. This signals no real change in his personality; Emma might as well still be alive.

When Emma dies and Randall plants forty-five acres of
sweet peas, he appears to have completely shaken his wife's
influence. The worried look upon his face seems understand-
able, considering the gamble Peter has taken. Therefore,

except for a few hints in the narrative to the contrary, Randall appears to be liberated from Emma's domination. The blue and pink sea of sweet pea blossoms becomes a symbol of his liberation. One would expect, therefore, that Peter is free to live the libidinous life of his fantasies. But this is not the case. The new, liberated Peter turns out to be none other than the old, slavish Peter. His shoulder harness and stomach belt serve only to suggest his more significant psychological bondage. We do not discover this, however, until the story's conclusion.

Since Emma appears for only a short time in the narrative, Steinbeck characterizes her quickly, but with abundant details. She is a forty-five year old, "skin-and-bones," proud matron whose "face was as wrinkled and brown as that of an old, old woman" (p. 111). Steinbeck oddly compares her to a bird: This "little skinny bird of a woman" has "dark, sharp bird eyes" (pp. 114-115). And like other wives in The Long Valley, Emma is childless. The Randall farmhouse is reflective of Emma: "clean and dusted," and "unscarred, uncarved, unchalked" (pp. 116, 113). Emma's house has the same "hard-swept" (p. 10) look as Elisa Allen's in "The Chrysanthemums." Similarly, each woman has a fenced yard, with a well-manicured garden, and their family farms are located "across the Salinas River, next to the foothills" (p. 112). The nearly identical setting in these two stories is no coincidence, for in the first manuscript version of "The Chrysanthemums," as mentioned above, Henry Allen (like Peter Randall) intends to plant sweet peas and is also upbraided by his wife for tracking dirt into the house.[66]

Ed Chappell, who like Emma appears infrequently, is instrumental in revealing three clues that Randall does not change after his wife's death. First, although claiming he will no longer wind the mantel clock whose "clack-clack-clack is too mournful" (p. 120), Randall keeps the clock running since its ticking suggests Emma's heartbeat. Second, despite his boast that he will "track dirt into the house" (p. 121) to trample upon his deceased wife's obsession with cleanliness, Randall continues to uphold her spick-and-span standards. And third, while he promises to hire a "big fat housekeeper" (p. 121)--his most rebellious plan, since Emma had adamantly "refused to hire a girl" (p. 112)--Randall never finds time to look for one. Ed Chappell carefully notes that none of these proposed changes is adopted. Each constitutes a hid-

den reminder of Emma's psychological domination over her
husband.

Another minor character almost as important as Ed
Chappell is expert farmer, Clark Dewitt. Although Dewitt
never actually appears in the story, his pronouncements
about the perils of growing sweet peas are given special
weight because he, along with Peter Randall, is one of the
valley's brightest farmers. Dewitt, like Chappell, is a device Steinbeck uses to place Randall in high relief. Without
the opinions and observations of these minor characters, the
third-person omniscient narrator would be left with the entire
burden of characterizing the story's protagonist. Finally,
"The Harness" is hardly the most artistically refined story
in the collection, yet its surprising conclusion reveals a
seemingly ordinary man to be psychologically complex, perhaps even profoundly disturbed.

"The Vigilante"
(1936)

and

"Case History"
(ca. 1934)

During the mid-1930s, Steinbeck became fascinated
with group or "mob" behavior. His interest in this phenomenon is especially evident in "The Vigilante." One night in
a small, California town, a man named Mike joins some vigilantes who storm a jail and lynch a black prisoner. After-
ward, as he walks from the dark scene towards a tavern,
Mike is overcome by loneliness. He brags to the bartender,
Welch, that he was the first into the jail and then displays
a piece of blue denim torn from the victim's body. Welch offers to buy the souvenir, and pours Mike a free beer. Soon
the two men close the bar and walk into a residential district.
Arriving at his home, Mike is badgered by his suspicious
wife, who accuses him of being with a woman. Rather than
denying this, he simply tells her to read the morning paper.
Nevertheless, when he looks in the mirror, Mike feels as if
he has been unfaithful.

"The Vigilante" is a brief (only "Breakfast" is shorter)
and a tightly-knit narrative. Although most critics contend

that the story focuses on the aftermath of the lynching and
Mike's reaction to it, Steinbeck devotes nearly one-half of
the tale to describing the hanging itself. True, when the
story opens, the black prisoner is already a dangling "blu-
ish grey" corpse (p. 133), yet how he comes to his demise is
fully recounted in a series of flashbacks. First, Mike recalls
struggling among the mob for a chance to pull the execution
rope (p. 134). Second, he remembers an earlier moment when
the vigilantes rushed the jail (p. 135). Third, Mike retells
the lynching incident in full to Welch, mentioning the sheriff's complicity and the gruesomeness of the prisoner's ab-
abduction (pp. 136-138). Finally, to complete this description of the events, Steinbeck has Mike speculate on how the
sheriff will "cut the nigger down and clean up some" (p.
138).

Steinbeck devotes slightly more than half of the narrative to Mike's response to the lynching. At first, Mike feels
heavy and unreal, and then ashamed. He slinks away from
the hanging, pulling "his cap down over his eyes" (p. 133).
But then his sense of human decency is aroused when the
mob puts a torch to the dead man's dangling feet. " 'That
don't do no good,'" he says. Ironically, Mike who has put
his body and soul into hanging a man, now quibbles over
the treatment of his corpse. Mike must justify his participation, so he agrees with an onlooker that tax dollars have
been saved by the gang-style murder (p. 134). As soon as
he leaves the crowd, Mike becomes desperately lonely and
rushes for the nearest bar. Once the bar closes Mike becomes lonely again, and shies away when Welch asks him
how the lynching made him feel. Mike merely replies that
he feels " 'satisfied ... but tired and kind of sleepy'" (p.
140). Thus, Mike responds to the hanging in different
ways. He feels weary, satisfied, ashamed, indignant, lonely, and proud.

Images of light and darkness in the story echo Mike's
feelings. Consistently, darkness to Mike means loneliness,
and light, the escape from loneliness. Thus, when the vigilante's torches are extinguished, Mike flees to a surer source
of light, the "burning neon word BEER" (p. 135) on the
nearby tavern. The illumination he finds there, however,
is short-lived. Soon Welch switches off the "red neon sign
and the house lights" (p. 139) and the two men step back
into the darkness. As they approach Mike's house, he says,

"'Look, there's light in the kitchen'" (p. 140). Although the glow from his kitchen window is no cause for celebration, it represents to Mike a beacon guiding him out of the darkness. Each time he leaves an illuminated area, such as the lynching site or Welch's bar, loneliness overtakes him. Hence, he always moves toward light with a sense of urgency.

As a native of the small town where the lynching occurs, Mike speaks with defective grammar (e.g., "'That don't do no good'") and seems unable to think for himself. Upon hearing the catchy phrase "'sneaky lawyers,'" for instance, he repeats it over and over again (pp. 134, 136). Mike's "thin, petulant" (p. 141) wife is suspicious, complaining, and apparently dissatisfied with her husband. And, like Elisa Allen and Mary Teller, she is childless. Welch, the bartender, is "small ... like an aged mouse ... unkempt and fearful" (p. 135). His furtive manner echoes that of the vigilantes who sneak silently away from the smoldering corpse. Curiously, Steinbeck describes the physical appearance of all the principal characters (even the corpse) except Mike, suggesting that he is an "average" man who behaves in this situation as any average man would. In fact, Mike (no last name) is the typical "unit man" Steinbeck has in mind when he explains the Phalanx Theory in his philosophical dialogue, "Case History."

Composed in the same copybook with "The Vigilante" and other short fiction of the 1930s, "Case History" is a 4,500-word narrative in which Steinbeck delivers perhaps his earliest and most comprehensive statement of the Phalanx, or "group-man," Theory.[67] According to this theory, a group is an individual with desires, hungers, and strivings of its own, and actually controls the behavior of the unit men who comprise it. Preceding this explanation of the Phalanx Theory, Steinbeck depicts a lynching nearly identical to that in "The Vigilante." John Ramsy (counterpart of Mike) joins a furious mob that smashes through the door of the Salinas jail and lynches a suspected child murderer. Later Ramsy explains his actions to Will McKay (counterpart of Welch) and proves himself to be neither a bigot, nor a racist, nor even a violent man; he merely longs to become part of the group. These two elements of the narrative--the lynching scene and its explanation--make "Case History" an essential document for understanding "The Vigilante."

Over the years critics (without apparent knowledge of
"Case History") have conjectured various reasons for Mike's
behavior in "The Vigilante": Warren French says that bore-
dom and a suspicious wife precipitate Mike's violent actions;
Franklin E. Court attributes the protagonist's behavior to
the inescapable futility of his life; Brian Barbour suggests
unrest of the soul and repressed sexual desire; Antoni
Gajewski simply calls Mike the "average American racist."[68]
Peter Lisca believes that "The vigilante, like the grandfather
in 'The Leader of the People,' fully lives only for that time
when he is part of the group"; and, similarly, Richard Astro
contends that although lynching is "something unreal and
foreign to his basic nature," Mike forgets himself and is
swallowed up by the mob.[69]

Steinbeck's explanation of Phalanx behavior in "Case
History" parallels the arguments of Lisca and Astro on "The
Vigilante." Through Ramsy, Steinbeck says that the unit
man, regardless of his individual disposition, always yearns
to join the group. Within him is a keying mechanism linked
to the Phalanx. Consequently, when the group calls him,
the unit man quickly responds. This, then, is the under-
lying reason why Mike becomes "The Vigilante"--not primarily because he is sexually frustrated, bored, or a racist,
but because he longs to attach himself to the group.

"Johnny Bear"
(1937)

Steinbeck's unusual short story, "Johnny Bear," has
less to do with its huge, moronic titular character, than with
the village of Loma whose symbols of respectability he top-
ples. Johnny Bear is an anthropoidal half-wit who begs
whiskey from patrons at the Buffalo Bar. When anyone buys
him a drink, he rewards his benefactor by mimicking voices
he has overheard. One evening the narrator, a worker from
a nearby dredging barge, hears Johnny Bear repeating the
conversation of a man and a woman. The man's voice is that
of the narrator himself, and the woman's, his date on a recent evening, Mae Romero. This performance embarrasses
everyone in the bar, especially the narrator. To earn another whiskey, Johnny Bear then utters the voices of two
women, one reprimanding the other for her unbridled pas-
sions. The words are those of Emalin and Amy Hawkins,

the town's aristocrats. On a later night, Johnny Bear mimics
the sisters' voices again, this time revealing that Amy has
attempted to hang herself. Everyone in the bar is dumb-
struck. After a few days, Johnny Bear discloses that Amy
is pregnant by a Chinese man and has committed suicide.
Buffalo Bar patrons are ashamed, for Loma's first ladies
have been disgraced.

Peter Lisca rightly argues that the central focus of
"Johnny Bear" is the fallen Hawkins sisters, rather than the
strange cretin who reveals their unexpected behavior.
Lisca contends that the tale exposes a "social group ... and
the conflict between its innate curiosity and its desire to
perpetuate the symbols of its decorum."[70] Although this
may be the story's central interest, "Johnny Bear" contains
several lesser, sometimes competing interests. The two most
prominent are the swamp dredger with its crew, and the
character, Johnny Bear.

The swamp dredger subplot in the story has its origin
in Steinbeck's own experience. Nelson Valjean explains that
Steinbeck once worked on a dredger "draining lakes and
canals near Castroville," California. Castroville, today called
by residents the artichoke capital of the world, was Steinbeck's model for the town of Loma. When employed on the
dredger, Steinbeck frequently "ate at the little Bennett
Hotel," the counterpart of Mrs. Ratz's house in the story.[71]
While his ability to particularize this setting lends the town
an air of reality, Steinbeck's frequent references to the
swamp dredger detract from the tale's artistic unity. The
dredger's succession of cooks, its unfortunate spate of ac-
cidents--when one worker loses both legs and another develops blood poisoning (p. 162)--and the unabated (except
Sundays) drone of its diesel engine, become random details
cluttering the plot.

The second competing element in the story is Johnny
Bear himself. The origins of this bizarre creature probably
stem from an incident described by Steinbeck's Stanford
classmate and friend, Webster Street:

> One day we were coming back from Palo Alto on
> the way to Salinas and we stopped for a beer at a
> bar just outside Castroville. We were sitting there
> talking, and suddenly we heard the bartender speaking

to somebody wearing bib overalls. We listened for
a while. The bartender said, "And then what did
you do?" and the guy went through all sorts of mo-
tions. He didn't talk with his fingers as in sign
language, rather he illustrated what he did. He
was mute, he could hear but could not speak. I'm
certain that John based the story of "Johny Bear"
(sic) on that episode. As a matter of fact, on the
way back he said, "Did you pay attention to that
fella, the guy in the overalls? You know he could
do a lot of harm, that guy."[72]

Steinbeck keeps Johnny Bear so clearly in view during
the narrative that Edmund Wilson has mistaken him for the
protagonist.[73] Called by the narrator, "just a kind of recording and reproducing device, only you use a glass of
whiskey instead of a nickel" (p. 164), Johnny Bear is another of Steinbeck's "subnormal" characters, such as Lennie
in Of Mice and Men (1937) and Tularecito in Pastures of
Heaven (1932). But Johnny Bear has a distinctive gift: he
can duplicate exactly the words and the voice of anyone he
hears. That patrons of the Buffalo Bar will pay him in shots
of whiskey if he repeats what he has heard is motivation
enough for this hulking man. Silently he moves about Loma,
eavesdropping on unsuspecting citizens. Peter Lisca equates
his capacity as a recording device with "the artist's role in
society.... Johnny Bear holds the mirror up to mankind and
reveals through his mimetic talent the hidden festers of society."[74] In this way, he embarrasses the story's narrator and
exposes the secrets of the Hawkins family. Even given Johnny
Bear's strange appearance and antics, he cannot function as
a protagonist, as Wilson suggests, because he does not act;
he only duplicates the words and actions of others, particularly the story's more likely protagonists--Amy and Emalin
Hawkins.

Amy Hawkins' affair and Emalin's response to it actually provide enough material for a separate story. But Steinbeck uses this material in "Johnny Bear" to demonstrate how
the fall of a "respectable" family can send shock waves
through a narrow community like Loma. In Emalin and Amy,
Steinbeck creates an early version of the Cain-Abel relationships (e.g., Charles-Adam, Cathy-Adam, Caleb-Aron, and
Caleb-Abra) in East of Eden (1952). In these relationships
one individual is usually soft, sensitive, warm, compassionate,

and understanding, while the other is cold, stern, calculating, and sometimes diabolical. Thus, when Amy's mid-life passion is excited by a Chinese share-cropper, Emalin tells her sister that she would be better dead than to indulge it (p. 153). When Amy inquires if her sister has ever felt such yearnings, Emalin replies, "'if ever I had, I would cut that part of me away'" (p. 153). Then after Amy's suicide, Emalin appeals to the doctor in a cold, controlled voice, "'Can you make out a certificate without mentioning'" [Amy's pregnancy]? Emalin's concern for the family reputation blinds her to Amy's needs. In fact, the doctor even suggests Emalin's complicity in the suicide (p. 166).

The Hawkins' horse and buggy provide an apt metaphor for Emalin's struggle to uphold rigid moral standards. The horse is harnessed in blinders and a "check-rein" that is entirely "too short for such an old horse" (p. 157). The blinders suggest narrow-mindedness. The short check-rein which prohibits the horse from lowering its neck implies the strict, even unhealthy rules of conduct Emalin applies to herself and Amy. Emalin expects Amy to remain fixed in a "respectable" moral posture--as Emma Randall expects of her husband in "The Harness." This forced compliance causes severe repercussions: Peter Randall becomes haunted and emotionally disturbed; Amy Hawkins commits suicide.

Steinbeck uses apt imagery to stress the moral murkiness of Loma. He notes "its fogs, with its great swamp like a hideous sin ..." (p. 158). This fog imagery recurs frequently: "nasty fog" (p. 148), "evil-smelling fog" (p. 154), "slow, squirming mist" (p. 155), and finally the narrator says, "It seemed to me that that fog was clinging to the cypress hedge of the Hawkins' house ... fog balls were clustered about it and others were slowly moving in" (p. 164). Then he suggests the fog's meaning: "I smiled as I walked along at the way a man's thought can rearrange nature to fit his thoughts" (p. 164). In other words, he senses doom hanging over the Hawkins' house, the fog piling up upon their cypress hedge signifying this doom, as well as the Hawkins sisters' attempt to conceal it.

In addition to the fog imagery, Steinbeck makes subtle comments about the Hawkins sisters and others in Loma through his descriptions of their dwellings. The most unusual feature of the Hawkins' house is its "incredibly thick

and strong" hedge (p. 156). The narrator calls it a high
"green barrier" (p. 156) which suggests that the Hawkins
sisters either desire exclusiveness or they have something
to conceal. The story's surprise ending reveals that both
assumptions are correct. Another curious feature about
their home is its tan paint and dark brown trim, a color
"combination favored for railroad stations and schools in
California" (p. 156). Thus, even though concealed, the
Hawkins' home assumes the aura of a public building, a public institution, or as Alex Hartnell calls it: "'The safe thing
... [t]he place where a girl can get reassurance'" (p. 163).

Steinbeck's description of the village itself is most revealing. The Methodist church stands at the "highest place
on the hill" (p. 146). This most visible edifice--its spire
can be seen for miles--suggests the church's influence in
the community. However, the influence Steinbeck seems to
have in mind is not necessarily a good one. The populace
of Loma lives in "small wooden houses" (p. 146) and the
land owners live on "small yards usually enclosed by high
walls of clipped cypress ...," suggesting narrow,
cramped lives. Steinbeck says there is "nothing to do in
Loma" (p. 146).

The only real communion that takes place occurs not in
the Methodist Church or the Masonic Hall, but in the bar--
"'[T]he Buffalo Bar is the mind of Loma'" (p. 158). Here attitudes are molded and reinforced over shots of whiskey.
"[P]osters and cards and pictures stuck to the wall" of the
Buffalo Bar reflect the retarded consciousness of the community (p. 147). These announcements contain appeals by
political candidates, salesmen, and auctioneers, some of whom
have been dead for years. The bar itself is an uncomfortable
place with a "bare wood" floor and "hard and straight" chairs
(p. 146). Fat Carl, the bartender, utters his stock response
to regulars and strangers alike: "'What'll it be?'" (p. 147).
His repetitive phrase illustrates the torpor that has stolen
over Loma.

The story's surprise ending suggesting that Amy's
liaison is doubly degrading since it involves a Chinese man--
a "Chink" (p. 157)--does not represent the kind of thinking
we like to remember Steinbeck for.[75] Nor does the narrator's
relationship with Mae Romero, the "pretty half-Mexican girl"
(p. 148) with whom he has "scraped an acquaintance" (pp.

147-8). When one night in the Buffalo Bar Johnny Bear
recites the narrator's advances on Mae, he sighs, "I was
cravenly glad Mae Romero had no brothers. What obvious,
forced, ridiculous words had come from Johnny Bear" (p.
149). Alex Hartnell explains to his friend: " 'If you're
worrying about Mae's reputation, don't. Johnny Bear has
followed Mae before' " (p. 150). Alex implies that Mae is
disreputable, yet Buffalo Bar regulars find nothing wrong
with the narrator's advances. By Loma's standards, a white
male may seduce a non-white female with impunity. However,
when a white woman (Amy Hawkins) has an affair with a
Chinese share-cropper, she is thought a disgrace to the
community. These rather unsavory attitudes, which may be
more of a sign of the times than of Steinbeck's sensibility,
make "Johnny Bear" one tale that does not entirely reflect
well on its author.

"The Murder"
(1934)

        Steinbeck's first short story to receive a national
prize--the O. Henry Memorial Award of 1934--was "The Murder." In the tale California rancher Jim Moore marries a
Yugoslavian girl whose ways are foreign to his own. Jelka
Sepic becomes a dutiful wife, if not a good companion. Ig-
noring his father-in-law's admonition that Jelka will love only
a man who beats her, Jim fails to develop a satisfying intima-
cy with her and instead begins to visit the Three Star brothel
in Monterey. One Saturday evening on the trail to Monterey,
a neighbor informs Jim that one of his calves has been killed
by rustlers. Jim doubles back and arrives home to find Jelka
in bed with her male cousin. After giving it a moment's
thought, Jim aims his rifle between the cousin's eyes and
fires. Once the murder charge is dismissed by a deputy
sheriff, Jim flogs his wife bloody with a bull whip. Rather
than revolt, Jelka smiles, becomes more personable, and
lovingly fries her husband a breakfast of eggs and bacon.

        As was his custom in stories written during the 1930s,
Steinbeck begins "The Murder" with an extended description
of the setting. The atmospheric details he emphasizes in
most tales of the period bear on plot, theme, or character.
In "The Chrysanthemums," as we have seen, the fog which
shrouds the Salinas Valley like a closed pot reflects Elisa

Allen's spiritual frustration. The grey colors of winter, the
absence of sunlight, and the cold air all suggest her condition and reinforce the story's theme. In such other Long
Valley stories as "The White Quail" and "Flight" the settings
have similarly significant implications. In "The Murder,"
however, this correspondence between setting and other elements in the narrative breaks down. Steinbeck painstakingly
describes a "stone castle" and an old ranch house, creaking
and rusting below it, but then never brings these back into
the story again.

Roy S. Simmonds explains the reason for this incongru-
ity between the setting and other formal qualities of the tale:
"In the manuscript of 'The Murder' Steinbeck initially set the
story in the Corral de Tierra [fictional setting of The Pastures of Heaven] but subsequently, while the work was still
in its primary manuscript stage, changed the setting to the
Valle del Castillo...."[76] Even though Steinbeck tried to dis-
guise the Pastures landscape, it emerges nevertheless. "At
the head of the canyon there stands a tremendous stone castle...." (p. 171). With these words Steinbeck describes a
natural rock formation which towers above the old Moore ranch
house abandoned when Jim Moore built a new home farther
down the canyon. In real life this precipice stands over the
Corral de Tierra and is called by local residents "the Castle."[77]

In plot structure, as in setting, "The Murder" resembles
several stories in The Pastures of Heaven--principally because
of the surprise entrance of Moore's neighbor, George, who
tips off Moore about a dead calf found with his brand on it.
George's intrusion leading Jim to discover his wife with her
lover is an obvious device reminiscent of the Munroe's inter-
ventions in Pastures. By encountering George on the trail
to Monterey, Jim Moore's illusions about Jelka's fidelity are
shattered, as is his mistaken assumption that he can treat
his Yugoslavian wife like any American woman. Moore quickly recovers from his disillusionment and alters his behavior.
He beats his wife, causing her to hold him in higher esteem.
This beating solves both Jelka's problems and Jim's. Jelka
now has a husband who treats her as (she thinks) a Yugoslavian wife should be treated. And with Jelka's new respon-
siveness to her husband, Jim may no longer need his weekly
visits to the Three Star brothel in Monterey. The solution
is as absurdly simply as it is unpalatable.

Jim Moore, who thrashes his wife and murders her
cousin, is another of Steinbeck's nondescript male protagonists. Like Mike in "The Vigilante" and Peter Randall in
"The Harness," Moore's physical appearance remains shrouded.
Nevertheless, Steinbeck's sketch of him evokes an aura of
masculinity; his manly beard at age thirty and his purchase
of a Guernsey bull contribute to this aura. Steinbeck describes Jelka, in contrast to Jim, with lavish detail. Sometimes she resembles an animal, with "eyes as large and ques-
tioning as a doe's eyes" (p. 172). She whimpers with pleasure at Jim's touch (p. 174) and whines like a puppy when he
attacks her with a bull whip (p. 185).

But it is not Jelka's apparent animal quality that sepa-
rates her from Jim, (Jim realizes "that he could not get in
touch with her in any way" [p. 174]). Rather, culture and
heritage divide the two. Only after Jim catches Jelka in an
adulterous affair does he realize how wide this gap is, and
then he quickly determines to narrow it. As a result, he alters what he considers the traditional role of a husband, and
flogs Jelka. Robert Murray Davis suggests that Steinbeck
focuses not on the physical action in the story, but on the
psychological--specifically, "Jim's becoming a satisfactory husband and complete human being."[78] In the end, Jim accepts
principles foreign to his own--namely his father-in-law's
counsel to physically abuse Jelka. Jim's changed behavior,
though violent, suggests a certain humility and an understanding that his American way of doing things is not always
the best. His slaying of her cousin, on the other hand,
smacks of pure machismo.

Steinbeck's description of the shooting is remarkably
graphic. With a few details he brings the scene into crisp
focus: "Jim cocked the rifle. The steel click sounded
through the house.... The front sight wavered a moment
and then came to rest.... The gun crash tore the air.
Jim, still looking down the barrel, saw the whole bed jolt
under the blow" (p. 183). This passage illustrates the in-
carnation of a powerful emotion: the jealous husband's urge
to kill his spouse's lover. The significance of the slaying
is heightened since it seems to be Jim's way to vent his
frustration over Jelka's foreignness. The cathartic effect of
Jim's crime, therefore, is immense. No doubt judges for the
O. Henry Memorial Award noticed this, and especially Steinbeck's breathtaking description of the crucial scene.

"Saint Katy the Virgin"
(1936)

Generally recognized as an anomaly among Steinbeck's
Long Valley stories, "Saint Katy the Virgin" represents a
generic blend of the saint's life, beast fable, fabliau, and
farce. Roark, a bad man who lives in the County of P___
in the year 13__, tithes his depraved pig, Katy, to Brothers
Paul and Colin. When Paul slips a cord through Katy's nose
ring to lead her away, she takes a bite out of Colin's leg.
Paul kicks Katy in the snout, increasing her ire. She chases
both monks up a thorn tree, and waits underneath pacing
back and forth. Paul soon lowers an iron crucifix and dan-
gles it in front of her, which miraculously exorcises the devil
from her. Upon arriving at the monastery with the redeemed
pig, Paul and Colin are reprimanded by Father Benedict,
since Katy--now a coverted Christian--cannot be slaughtered.
Katy's life henceforth becomes saintly. She heals the af-
flicted and blesses the multitudes, so that posthumously she
is added to the Calendar of the Elect and her bones become
holy relics able to cure female troubles and ringworm.

Most critics have questioned this odd addition to a collection of stories whose primary subject is purportedly the
lives of Salinas Valley people during the 1930s. Among these
tales which are homogeneous in milieu, a bawdy, farcical beast
fable or saint's life does not seem to belong. Consequently,
Joseph Fontenrose calls "Saint Katy" a "maverick in the collection." Brian Barbour, as noted above, says that the
story's appearance in The Long Valley shows Steinbeck's
"lack of critical judgment." And Warren French simply labels
the tale "conspicuously different in content and tone."[79] Why
did Steinbeck include it? He did so, according to Sanford E.
Marovitz, at the request of Pat Covici, then editor of Covici-
Friede, the house slated to publish The Long Valley. Covici
had no doubt been heartened by the rapid disappearance of
the story's first edition printed privately as a monograph,
"signed and limited to 199 copies." Since that monograph
was so well received, Steinbeck "willingly complied with his
agent's request to bring the satirical tale back into print,"
a tale the author had "dashed off chiefly as an entertainment
for himself."[80]

Although Steinbeck placed "Saint Katy the Virgin" near
the end of The Long Valley, he wrote it first (ca. May, 1932),

more than a year before he composed his next story, "The
Gift" (ca. June, 1933). Warren French suggests that "Saint
Katy" may have existed even prior to 1932, "since it is written in the mannered, facetious style [Steinbeck] abandoned
with the coming of the depression." Says French, the story
also reflects an "attitude toward conventional religiosity"
much like that expressed in Cup of Gold (1929) and To a
God Unknown (1933).[81] For like other Steinbeck stories
whose title characters are animals, Katy (the pig) serves to
point out the failings of humanity, especially religious hypoc-
risy. Through Katy, a profane, opportunistic side to monas-
tic life shows through. Edmund Wilson underscores this
point, saying that the result of the story "is not to dignify
the animal ... but to make human religion ridiculous."[82]

The somewhat grotesque character, Roark, seems to be
identified with this animal protagonist. Called by the narrator a "bad man," Roark transforms Katy from a docile piglet
into a vicious sow. Both pig and master continue in their
depraved ways until Katy's conversion, when Roark, too, is
miraculously reformed: "From that day on, he was no longer
a bad man; his whole life was changed in a moment" (p. 196).
If Steinbeck meant anything by this identification between
Roark and Katy, he neglected to develop it. Once Brothers
Paul and Colin lead Katy to their monastery, Roark slips out
of the story forever.

The brothers themselves are contrasting stereotypes of
clergymen, a pairing to be found in Chaucer's Canterbury
Tales. Paul (compare St. Paul) is an ascetic, idealized
brother resembling the young clerk riding with Chaucer's
pilgrims. Paul is a "thin, strong man, with a thin strong
face and a sharp eye." Colin, fittingly, is a "short round
man with a wide round face," who looks forward to "trying
the graces of God" right here on earth (p. 192). Like the
identification between Roark and Katy, Steinbeck does no
more than establish these contrasting traits between Paul and
Colin. Marovitz suggests that Steinbeck may have changed
"the emphasis and direction of his story as he wrote." This
hypothesis, if correct, explains why seemingly important
threads of the plot are introduced and then simply dropped--
the Roark-Katy and Paul-Colin relationships, for example.

Marovitz offers three tentative allegorical readings of
the tale: the first concerning topical issues in Monterey and

Pacific Grove; the second national social and economic woes; and the third a veiled blast against organized religion. But whether the story is read as a beast fable or an allegory, or both, Steinbeck's satiric intent is clear. Institutionalism had been the target of his college satires, but in "Saint Katy the Virgin" he turns his attention from university administrators to the Christian clergy. Chief among his indictments is the clergy's tendency to ignore facts which contradict their view of reality. For instance, a "sow with a litter is nevertheless canonized as a virgin."[83] Even without the benefit of these thinly veiled jabs at the church, "Saint Katy the Virgin" is a humorous, earthy tale. Yet some readers have puzzled over the story, and found it irrelevant or even offensive. Speaking for them, Elmer Davis concludes: "Saint Katy" is a "burlesque hagiography which might better have been left in private circulation."[84]

THE RED PONY STORIES
(1933-1936)

Introduction

Steinbeck's well-known story cycle, The Red Pony, focuses on the theme of initiation or (in Steinbeck's words) how a "child becomes a man." Steinbeck believed that facing death brings about "the first adulthood of any man or woman," and in these stories he attempted to depict this painful process.[85] Steinbeck himself was surrounded by impending death when he wrote the first of the four Red Pony stories. It was summer, 1933, and Olive Hamilton Steinbeck, the author's mother, was succumbing to a fatal illness. During the ordeal, Steinbeck reminisced with his father "about earlier days," especially "John's boyhood acquisition of his chestnut pony."[86] Perhaps these memories took the author back to a happier phase of his life, a time to which he no doubt gladly escaped. He wrote to George Albee:

> I don't know whether I told you that mother is now paralysed and will linger perhaps a year. It has been a bad time.... I have to fight an atmosphere of blue fog so thick and endless that I can see no opening in it.[87]

Steinbeck was apparently bracing himself for his first
encounter with the death of a loved one. Jody Tiflin undergoes a similar ordeal when his beloved red pony dies. Steinbeck focuses on the progress of Jody's initiation into the
reality of death by maintaining a consistent third-person
point of view, written from the boy's perspective, while seldom entering his mind. This restrained, objective treatment
keeps Jody, as well as the other characters, at a comfortable
distance from the reader. Yet, at the same time, Steinbeck's
graphic descriptions of suffering, violence, and death tend
to draw us close to the action. These seemingly contradic-
tory techniques result in what T.K. Whipple calls "the middle
distance," where "we feel the appropriate emotions--pity,
sympathy, terror and horror even--but with the delightful
sense that we are apart."[88]

The characters themselves are warmly human and believable. Says Arthur Mizener, "We are wholly convinced by
Jody's feelings for the life of nature and by its culmination
in his love for his red pony and his grief at its death."[89]
Other characters, too, are equally compelling: Billy Buck,
the old man--Gitano, and Jody's pioneering grandfather, not
to mention Gabilan the pony, Nellie the mare, and Doubletree
Mutt--Jody's rambunctious dog.

Critics almost invariably praise the four thematically
linked stories which comprise The Red Pony--"The Gift"
(1933), "The Great Mountains" (1933), "The Promise" (1937),
and "The Leader of the People" (1936). Mizener, as we have
seen, credits this collection with "an integrity, a responsibility to experience and a consequent unity of surface and symbol that Steinbeck has never achieved since." Brian Barbour
calls it "a successful tale" containing some of "Steinbeck's
most deeply felt work." Warren French lauds the series as
"one of his works in which form and content are most perfectly integrated."[90] The Red Pony, in sum, comprises some
of Steinbeck's most successful stories. Its flowing, episodic
structure, autobiographical themes, and objective point of
view make this story cycle deserving of the almost universal
praise it has received. Each of the four tales are discussed
below, beginning with "The Gift."

"The Gift"
(1933)

"The Gift" (originally entitled "The Red Pony") is the
short story that, by some estimates, launched Steinbeck's
career. Appearing in the November, 1933 issue of the North
American Review, it was his first work accepted by a prominent national magazine. As a result, readers across the
country suddenly became acquainted with the rising American author, John Steinbeck. "The Gift" is also noteworthy
for its unusual length. At about ten thousand words, it is
twice as long as the typical Long Valley selection, and perhaps the longest short story Steinbeck wrote.[91]

The tale concerns the first stages of Jody Tiflin's initiation into the adult world. After breakfast one summer
morning, rancher Carl Tiflin surprises his ten-year-old son,
Jody, with a gift of a red pony. Jody names the colt Gabilan, and eagerly awaits the day when he can ride it. With
cowhand Billy Buck's help, he begins to halter train and
later to saddle Gabilan. One clear morning Jody leaves him
in the corral, for Billy promises to lead the pony into the
barn in case of rain. When later that day it pours, Jody
runs home after school to find Gabilan standing in the corral, soaking wet. Although the guilt-ridden Billy insists
the rain will not harm Gabilan, the pony becomes dreadfully
ill. Billy's ministrations proving futile, Gabilan's condition steadily worsens. Near death one night, the pony wanders out of the barn. Jody, spotting it the next morning
encircled by buzzards, fails to revive Gabilan. The red
pony is dead.

In "The Gift," Jody's initiation into adulthood begins
by his learning three important lessons: human beings are
fallible; nature is uncaring and indifferent; and nature's im-
mutable law for all earthly creatures is death. Jody learns
his first lesson--that no mortal is perfect--when Billy Buck's
predictions for fair weather prove unreliable. The cowhand
then compounds his error by failing to shelter Gabilan during
the downpour, as he promised Jody he would. In the boy's
eyes, Billy's "hero image is tarnished."[92] But Jody learns
about human imperfection through his own negligent behavior
as well. Even though he resolves to care for his sick pony
through an entire night, sleep overtakes Jody. When he
awakens, he finds Gabilan lying outside the barn near death.

Through this tragic experience, Jody discovers that he cannot always control his actions. Realizing his own flaws, he
begins to accept human fallibility in others too. This marks
Jody's first significant step toward maturity.

Jody discovers nature's blank indifference to man--his
second lesson--when he sees a buzzard devouring the carcass
of his beloved Gabilan. The boy cannot fathom how this
winged predator of death has a legitimate place in nature.
In an attempt to combat the indifferent forces the bird represents, Jody grabs the buzzard before it can fly away and
beats it with a rock. But even while Jody is destroying the
vulture, its "red fearless eyes still looked at him, impersonal
and unafraid and detached" (p. 238). The buzzard's actions
and dying expression teach Jody "that nature is impersonal,
no respecter of human wishes."[93]

As he contemplates the buzzard's attack on Gabilan,
Jody learns his third lesson, that death is final and immuta-
ble. The pony's tragic end, says Howard Levant, propels
Jody into manhood; his developing awareness of death, in
other words, quickens the process of his maturity.[94] But
this ultimate lesson involves not just death, but a cycle of
both life and death, as illustrated by the change of seasons,
"the buzzards flying overhead, the life and death of Jody's
pony Gabilan, and the death of the buzzard Jody kills."[95]
These images suggesting a cycle of two seemingly antitheti-
cal principles underscore the dispiriting truth that even as
new life emerges, death reigns "invincible and final."[96]

Even before Gabilan dies and the buzzards swoop down
upon him, Jody has already grown and changed immensely.
A mischievous, somewhat irresponsible boy when the story
begins, he quickly reforms once Gabilan is put into his care.
Steinbeck foreshadows this metamorphosis when Jody hikes to
the "cold spring" at the brush line on the day before he receives the pony. The boy senses "an uncertainty in the air,
a feeling of change and of loss and of the gain of new and unfa-
miliar things" (p. 206). Because of the red pony, Jody matures rapidly; he leaps out of bed every morning to attend
to Gabilan, and becomes enthusiastic about his household
chores. Unfortunately, this enthusiasm wanes when the
pony approaches death. Jody arises more slowly--even
oversleeps--and forgets his chores. With Gabilan dreadfully ill, Jody again walks up to the brush line and sits "on

the edge of the mossy tub." When he looks down upon the
farm, "[t]he place was familiar, but curiously changed. It
wasn't itself any more, but a frame for things that were hap-
pening" (p. 235). Jody's two treks up to the brush line
bracket his growth and change. From the cold spring he
twice looks down upon the whitewashed ranch buildings,
seeing them each time with different eyes. As he matures,
therefore, familiar sights take on strange, new meanings.

Carl Tiflin and his wife play a lesser role in "The Gift"
than do Jody or Billy Buck. Steinbeck avoids physical descriptions of either Tiflin parent. Mrs. Tiflin, for example,
becomes merely an abstract, grey-headed mother figure (p.
203). Carl Tiflin is also given few physical attributes.
Steinbeck calls him "stern" (p. 204) and a "disciplinarian,"
yet also refers to him as "jovial" (p. 205). Billy Buck, of
course, shares center stage through much of the story with
Jody. In fact, Steinbeck begins "The Gift" with more than
a full-page description of Billy's physical appearance and his
early-morning activities. That Steinbeck introduces the cowhand at the very beginning of the story (a place the author
usually reserves for a description of setting) signifies Billy's
great importance.

Ultimately, it is Jody who gives the story unity and
appeal. As Steinbeck himself said of "The Gift," the narrative's effect "entirely depends upon the treatment." This
prompted Steinbeck to tell the story as though it came out of
the boy's mind, and to perceive the incidents through his
eyes. This is why the plot can seem so simple, yet by implication be so profound. Consequently, "The Gift" chal-
lenges both the adolescent and adult reader, for each finds
in the story a level of sophistication commensurate with his
or her intelligence and experience.

"The Great Mountains"
(1933)

Some critics of The Red Pony suggest that "The Great
Mountains" serves mainly as a calm interlude between the more
violent and dramatically intense stories, "The Gift" and "The
Promise."97 Owens argues, on the other hand, that it illustrates "the most central element in the moral awakening Jody
undergoes.... The blossoming of [his] questing impulse, his

desire to transcend the known and secure world" of the sunny Gabilan range to the east and broaching the unknowable, the
dark and mysterious "Great Ones" to the west.[98] Only half
the length of "The Gift," "The Great Mountains" takes place
during one twenty-four hour span and focuses on a single
event: the brief appearance of a venerable, dying Indian.
One afternoon Jody sees a lean, denim-clad old man approaching the ranchhouse who proclaims that he, Gitano, has returned to his birthplace to die. Carl Tiflin insists the old
man go away by morning. Nevertheless, Jody becomes fascinated by his reminiscence of a journey into the great mountains. Later when the boy and Gitano spot old Easter, the
Tiflins' ancient horse, Carl (tacitly comparing the animal to
Gitano) says that it ought to be shot. That night in the
bunkhouse, Jody visits the old man and marvels at his gleaming rapier. By morning Gitano has disappeared, and so has
Easter. Later in the day Carl learns that a decrepit horse
and rider were seen heading straight into the western mountains. When Jody looks upward and thinks he sees a dark
speck on a far ridge, the thought of Gitano, his rapier, and
the great mountains saddens him.

These mountains loom as the most ominous symbol in the
story. As we saw when discussing "Flight," Owens makes a
clear case for the Santa Lucias (coastal range) representing
death in Steinbeck's fiction.[99] To Jody they seem jagged,
dark, and savage, and always somewhat "impersonal,"
"aloof," and imperturbable (p. 242). When he compares the
"jolly" Gabilan mountains to the brooding "Great Ones,"
Jody shivers "a little at the contrast" (p. 242). They suggest, like Gitano and Easter, the unexplainable mystery of
death, a mystery Jody cannot fully comprehend. At the
story's end, Jody ascends again to the brush line as he did
in "The Gift," hoping to come to grips with the new feelings
stirring in him because of Gitano and the great mountains.
Whether Jody knows it or not, his "sympathies have been
broadened" by this experience.[100] A cruel and callous,
not to mention destructive young boy at the beginning of
the story, Jody grows as he contemplates the lesson he has
learned from the strange old man.

That lesson seems to be embodied in Gitano's "lovely
rapier" (p. 253). Ostensibly, the gleaming sword represents
the reverence Gitano still has for his father--from whom he
inherited the blade--and also the abiding dignity of Gitano's

own life and perhaps the mystery of his impending death. In
addition, Richard F. Peterson has argued that the rapier suggests a lance or spear from the Grail legend as discussed in
Jessie Weston's, From Ritual to Romance (1920); Gitano becoming a "Maimed King" and Jody a quester to restore his
wasted kingdom.[101] Unfortunately, Steinbeck does not clearly evoke these meanings with the sword itself. The boy's
awe over it, in consequence, seems melodramatic: "Jody
stood overwhelmed by the thing in Gitano's hand, a lean and
lovely rapier with a golden basket hilt.... It would be a
dreadful thing to tell anyone about it, for it would destroy
some fragile structure of truth (pp. 253-54). What this
sword has to do with truth and why Jody must keep its
knowledge to himself are questions Steinbeck raises but neglects to answer. Some of the "mystery" of Gitano's blade,
in other words, stems from its fuzziness as a symbol.

One symbol which in its application approaches allegory
is the decrepit thirty-year-old horse, Easter. Suggesting
useless old age (and, in contrast, resurrection), Easter becomes an obvious parallel to Gitano. In fact, the two ride
off as fellow sojourners into the mountains. But they not
only depart the Tiflin ranch in the same way, they also arrive in almost identical fashion. Both Gitano and Easter approach the ranch slowly "over the brow of the hill," and
both look exceedingly thin, with bones jutting out sharply
under their skin (pp. 243, 248). They seem to carry with
them the secret of death and a quiet dignity, as well.

In concluding "The Great Mountains," Steinbeck resorts
to a narrative technique he first tried in The Pastures of
Heaven, that of introducing one or more previously uninvolved
characters at the last moment to effect the story's conclusion.
As we have seen, the meddling Munroes act in this capacity
in several Pastures tales; and in the Long Valley tale, "The
Murder," a neighbor named "George" pops out of nowhere,
tipping off Jim Moore to some cattle rustlers and, inadver-
tently, to his unfaithful wife's lover. In "The Great Mountains," Steinbeck creates a similar character in Jess Taylor,
a neighboring rancher who also appears in "The Promise."
Taylor informs Carl Tiflin that Gitano has ridden away with
Easter. Despite this structural contrivance and an ambiguous symbol, "The Great Mountains" leaves us with much
to contemplate.

"The Promise"
(1937)

Although Steinbeck wrote "The Gift" and "The Great
Mountains" during the summer of 1933, he did not compose
"The Promise" until nearly a year later. One indication of
this lapse in time is the marked poetic quality of "The Promise." Imagery of color, vegetation, birds, animals, and the
seasons emerges prominently, as in such other 1934 stories
as "The Chrysanthemums" and "The White Quail." Through
these images in "The Promise," Steinbeck attempts to evoke
the mysteries of creation, birth, and death. That he does
so successfully is indicated by the story's inclusion in the
collection, O. Henry Memorial Award: Prize Stories of 1938.

One spring afternoon Carl Tiflin promises his son a
colt if he will work off the cost of breeding their mare, Nellie, and care for her during gestation. The next morning,
with a five dollar stud fee advanced by his father, Jody
walks Nellie to Jess Taylor's ranch. Before Jody and the
horse arrive, Taylor's black stallion, Sundog, breaks his
halter and charges toward them. Jody hides in the brush,
while the two animals violently mate. Taylor rescues the
frightened boy, and later sends Nellie and him on their way.
After several months, Nellie begins to swell. When her time
finally comes, she struggles painfully in labor. Realizing
that her foal is turned the wrong way, Billy Buck crushes
Nellie's skull with a hammer and then cuts open her stomach.
A slick black colt emerges. Billy lays the wet bundle at
Jody's feet and explains why he had to kill Nellie. Despite
the mare's death, the promise is fulfilled.

As in the previous Red Pony story, "The Promise"
chronicles the further initiation of Jody Tiflin. From the
tale's inception, Jody demonstrates that he is a changed
person. No longer mischievous and destructive, Jody has
become a gentle collector of horned toads, grasshoppers,
and newts. He has learned to respect and nurture forms of
life he previously destroyed. But central to Jody's continuing growth toward maturity in his opportunity to observe
animal procreation, from which he discovers that just as
death is sometimes violent (recall his pony, Gabilan), so too
is the creation of new life. He watches the wild and powerful black stallion, Sundog, kick Nellie and then bite her in

the neck until she oozes blood. With or without this fierce
energy, sexual knowledge is a crucial part of the adult world;
and, consequently, Jody's initiation must include it.[102] While
he waits nearly a year for Nellie to foal, Jody also learns the
virtue of patience. Finally, after the birth of this promised
colt--requiring Billy to kill the mare--Jody shares a sense of
guilt with the cowhand, whose "bloody face ... and haunted,
tired eyes" stick in the boy's mind.[103] From this experience
Jody becomes aware that "death and life are inseparably
bound together."[104]

        Steinbeck suggests their inseparability with two central
images: the black cypress where pigs are scalded and the
mossy green tub brimming with fresh, spring water. He re-
inforces these two with other imagery suggesting the cycle
of life and death, especially the changing of the seasons.
The story opens in the "green and gold" of spring, with its
cast of "silver" leaves, "blue" snakes, "yellow" grasshoppers, and "gold-" stomached horned toads (pp. 256-7). As
the narrative progresses through the year, Steinbeck rarely
misses an opportunity to brighten the story with seasonal
colors. With summer approaching, he evokes the "yellowing
hillsides" (p. 264). In the "warm bright autumn" he notes
that "the poison oak turned red" (p. 270). Finally, in winter he says that the hills "blackened" under the steady rain
(p. 273) and the nights became "black and thick" (p. 275),
so black that on the tragic dawn of Nellie's death, "no light
... penetrated into the cup of the ranch" (p. 277).

        Steinbeck also depicts the effect of seasonal changes on
the habits of birds and animals. When the story opens and
spring is in the air: a "green odor" lingers on the hillsides
spurring frenzied energy in horses, lambs, and "young clumsy calves" (p. 257). Nellie becomes "crazy as a coot" (p.
262). On fences, "blackbirds," "meadowlarks" and "wild
doves" sing with rejuvenated vigor (p. 262). Some of this
jubilation among both birds and animals seems to imply sexual
arousal, such as when Nellie, in heat, backs up against a
gate, "rubbing her buttocks on the heavy post" (p. 259;
261). Then ripening "wild oats" (p. 265) become a motif
suggesting Nellie's fertilization and pregnancy. For example,
as Jody leads Nellie to be bred with Sundog, the boy passes
"wild oats" along the road, "whose heads were just clearing
their scabbards" (p. 262). The phallic implication of these
"heads" is echoed by Sundog's "stiff, erected nostrils" (p.

263). Once Nellie is impregnated, Steinbeck again employs the "wild oat" image--this time to suggest the onerousness of gestation and birth. Like Nellie, "the wild oats were ripening. Every head bent sharply under its load of grain" (p. 265). Finally that Steinbeck intends the black stallion, Sundog, to evoke powerful, masculine qualities is evidenced by brilliant sunlight reflecting his glistening eyes and on his sleek, black hide. These bright spots of light, like the name "Sundog" itself, suggest the sun's warmth and creative energy.

Aside from this seasonal and sexual imagery, the most noticeable images in "The Promise" are the old, green tub and the black cypress. The first, a "thin stream of spring water [running] into an old green tub," obviously stands for life itself (p. 268); beyond this it suggests purification and perhaps even redemption. More importantly, as Jody's refuge during times of change and crisis, the stream of spring water brings to mind the "transitional phases of the life cycle."[105] The opposite and enemy of the green tub, says Steinbeck, is the "black cypress tree" (p. 268), where pigs are scalded in an iron kettle. The blackness of the cypress as well as the slaughter which occurs under its boughs suggest death. The cypress also brings to mind a tree of knowledge, and, paradoxically, a tree of life. There is no denying that Jody learns from the black cypress. In fact, his initiation depends upon his accepting the inevitability of dissolution and death. The old, dying, and dead surround Jody, and his knowledge of death through Gabilan, Gitano, Nellie, and his aged grandfather (in "The Leader of People") teaches him to respect and appreciate all forms of life. As a symbol of blackness and destruction, therefore, the black cypress further instructs Jody in the high cost of life--that ultimately life must be paid for by death.

"The Leader of the People"
(1936)

"The Leader of the People" shares the same setting and, except for the addition of Jody's grandfather, the same principal characters with the three previous Red Pony stories. The plot of this fourth tale, however, differs markedly from that of its counterparts. In addition to providing the final chapter in Jody's initiation into adulthood, Steinbeck

focuses on the sorrowful plight of a group man--the grand-
father--who has been divested of his group. When the old
man arrives at the Tiflin ranch for a brief visit, Jody invites him to hunt mice in a haystack. The grandfather expresses surprise that the new generation has gone soft and
resorted to hunting mice. That evening he fondly recalls
his adventures leading wagon trains across the prairies of
the old west. Carl Tiflin, having heard these "westering"
stories many times before, cruelly reminds his father-in-law
that he is repeating himself. At the urging of Jody, however, the tales continue. The next morning before the
grandfather arrives at breakfast, Carl again complains about
his stories. Silently, the old man walks in and overhears.
Carl sheepishly apologizes. Later, the grandfather tells
Jody that the spirit of "westering" has died out in the people, and that his role in the westward movement has lost its
meaning. Jody sympathetically fixes his grandfather a glass
of lemonade.

    In "The Leader of the People," the grandfather's ex-
perience of heading a group of settlers is surprisingly similar to the group experiences of protagonists in two other
stories Steinbeck also composed in 1934: Mike in "The Vigilante" and John Ramsy in the unpublished "Case History."
Both Mike and Ramsy revel in their memories of the group
to which they were once attached--Mike a lynching mob and
Ramsy an infantry platoon. These two protagonists and the
grandfather have much in common; after their exposure to
the group or "phalanx," everyday life no longer fulfills
them.[106] They survive only on nostalgia for their lost
group, and relish those few moments when they can recount
the phalanx experience to willing (or in grandfather's case,
unwilling) listeners. Jody's grandfather is buoyed by his
recollections of riding at the head of a giant phalanx, "a
whole bunch of people made into one big crawling beast"
(p. 302). Consequently, he looms very large in the story.
Jody's initiation, clearly the dominant theme in the previous
Red Pony tales, must vie in "The Leader of the People" with
this new element introduced by the grandfather: stories of
an immense phalanx of humanity moving west, or as he puts
it, "westering."

    Some critics have faulted the story for this. To them,
the grandfather's preoccupation with "westering" interferes
with Jody's initiation. Donald Houghton argues that the

grandfather's explanation of westering "comes upon us suddenly and apparently has no reference to anything else
which happens in this story or in The Red Pony.... [It] is
an unfortunate, confusing, and unnecessary digression which
tears at the emotional and thematic unity of the story."[107]
Robert Morsberger counters Houghton, saying that "westering" is "the crucial experience" in grandfather's generation,
and hence "is not a digression that should be cut but the
basis of the generation gap" between Jody and the old man.
Morsberger explains that grandfather's stories about the
crossing comprise another lesson in Jody's continuing initiation, exposing the boy to his ancestor's heroic tradition.[108]
From this vantage point, Philip J. West argues that the grandfather resembles a bard transmitting oral history to the new
generation, (i.e. Jody).[109]

    If "westering" is truly "the crucial experience" of the
grandfather's era, as Morsberger suggests, then the old
man's reminiscences about it certainly do serve to bridge the
generation gap and promote Jody's initiation. However, we
need to distinguish between occasions when the grandfather
acts as a purveyor of oral history and other times when he
becomes merely a spokesman for Steinbeck's theory of the
phalanx. As we have seen, this theory provides that a
group is a living entity with desires, hungers, and strivings of its own, and actually controls the units that comprise it. In addition, the group as a single organism (rather
than as individual members) chooses its leader based on its
immediate needs. In his day, grandfather became the head
of a phalanx, but as he concedes to Jody, "[I]f I hadn't been
there, someone else would have been the head. The thing
had to have a head" (p. 302). This same principle applies
to Steinbeck's other stories involving group behavior, particularly the unpublished "Case History," where among a mob
John Ramsy finds himself suddenly at the head of a battering
ram bursting through the door of the Salinas jail.

    With this definition in mind, let us divide the grand-
father's tales into the two categories mentioned above: first,
when he speaks as a purveyor of oral history, and, second,
when he acts as a mouthpiece for Steinbeck's theory of the
phalanx. All of grandfather's tales leading up to the conclusion of the story amount to oral history, in which he recounts the lore of wagon trains on the prairie. He loves to
tell these stories, as evidenced by their frequency in the

in the text. First, upon meeting Jody, he recalls how troops
commonly hunted Indians, shot their children, and burst
teepees (p. 291). Second, he reminisces how during the
crossing he consumed nearly "five pounds of buffalo meat
every night" (p. 293). Then he remembers the time the
hunters found no game at all, and were unable to "even shoot
a coyote" (p. 294). Finally, he recounts how Indians often
attacked the circle of wagons, but the brave settlers crouched
under the wagons and fought back. Though these tales are
somewhat crude, they nevertheless relate to a common subject,
hunting, and connect the grandfather's tales with an important motif in the story: Jody's mice hunt.

While the grandfather's stories of the western crossing
fit thematically into "The Leader of the People," his closing
remarks about "the big crawling beast" do not. Here the
old man changes roles from a transmitter of oral history to a
spokesman for Steinbeck's theory of the phalanx. A clue
that his final comments on "westering" represent an abrupt
turn in the direction of the narrative is the altered image of
himself the grandfather presents. Through his earlier remi-
niscenses, he evokes the image of a great and stalwart leader. After hearing his stories, in fact, Jody imagines his
grandfather "on a huge white horse, marshaling the people"
(p. 297). Here Steinbeck depicts the old man as fearless,
sagacious, and heroic--a true leader of the people. In the
story's conclusion, however, the author shows his protagonist to be not so much a leader, as a mere figurehead. To
recall the grandfather's own words: "[I]f I hadn't been there,
someone else would have been the head. The thing had to
have a head" (p. 302). In addition, there are no links from
this last speech to anything that comes before it. Because
of this, the entire hunting motif, including the grandfather's
tales of soldiers, Indians, and buffalos comes to no end.
One of the story's dominant symbols--the "plump, sleek, ar-
rogant mice"--which contributes to the hunt motif and the
theme of degeneracy implied by the grandfather's comparison
between his generation and the present one, also has no connection with the old man's description of the phalanx. Thus,
from an heroic wagon train leader in the tradition of the wild
west to a mere figurehead fronting a giant phalanx, the
grandfather's changed image distances him from these important motifs in the story.

Finally, because the grandfather is clearly the tale's

protagonist, Jody's continuing initiation into adulthood slips
into the background; except for his unselfish show of sympathy for grandfather at the story's end, the subtle nuances
of the boy's growth toward maturity are overshadowed by the
grandfather and his conflict with Carl Tiflin. Because of
Carl's narrow-mindedness and cruelty, he shows himself to
be resentful, insensitive, and nearly devoid of human emotion.[110] Billy Buck, on the other hand, again emerges as a
hero, or as the grandfather says, "one of the few men of
the new generation who [has] not gone soft" (p. 292). But
the Tiflin family and Billy Buck fade into the background
while the grandfather tells his stories of Indians and wagon
trains--stories which fit organically into the narrative until
their subject becomes Steinbeck's phalanx theory. Conse--
quently, "The Leader of the People" fails to achieve a syn-
thesis and resolution of its various themes, symbols, and
motifs. Yet the grandfather's "westering" foreshadows Steinbeck's most famous novel, The Grapes of Wrath (1939), whose
interchapters will be appraised next.

INTERCALARY CHAPTERS IN
THE GRAPES OF WRATH
(1939)

A well-known American classic, The Grapes of Wrath
has been the subject of numerous articles and collections of
essays. Although usually treated as an indivisible whole,
more than half of the novel's thirty chapters are intercalary
pieces--"interchapters"--some of which like "Breakfast" (discussed above) Steinbeck published separately as short fiction.
Mary Ellen Caldwell defines the intercalary chapters of The
Grapes of Wrath as those "which do not directly advance
the narrative of the Joad family, but which, intercalated
between the chapters of the narrative proper, give the narrative increased depth and broader significance."[111] Indeed,
while independent of the main narrative, these interchapters
provide important background material and set the tone
for the episodes which follow them.

Since the intercalary chapters in The Grapes of Wrath
are closely tied to the main narrative, and since they consist
generally of "impersonal, panoramic accounts of conditions
or social forces,"[112] few of them amount to what we normally

think of as complete short stories. In these brief pieces
Steinbeck seldom focuses on particular people; characters
remain anonymous and thus represent others like themselves
who might be expected to behave in similar ways. It is as
if Steinbeck pans a wide-angle lens across his fictional landscape in order to capture the general conditions of the people en masse. Some exceptions should be mentioned. In
intercalary Chapter Three Steinbeck particularizes a resolute
turtle to represent the spirit of endurance of the Joads and
thousands of other migrant families. In intercalary Chapter
Five, the tractor driver who knocks a farm house off its
foundation turns out to be Joe Davis, an acquaintance of the
family he has just rendered homeless.[113] And in Chapter
Fifteen, the anonymous chefs and waitresses of hamburger
stands along Route 66 become the particular characters, Al
and Mae.

In sum, although The Grapes of Wrath contains sixteen
pieces of short fiction (Chapters 1, 3, 5, 7, 9, 11, 12, 14,
15, 17, 19, 21, 23, 25, 27 and 29) related in some way to
the central narrative, most appear to be vividly descriptive
sketches with neither characters nor action particularized
enough to make them complete stories. While several interchapters have been published separately, most have appeared
as excerpts in anthologies devoted to specific themes. One
such anthology, The Great Depression, edited by David A.
Shannon, includes an excerpt from The Grapes of Wrath entitled "The Okies." Another anthology designed for fresh-
men English courses includes the intercalary sketch about the
persistent turtle mentioned above.[114] Other Steinbeck novels
of the 1930s have been similarly excerpted as short fiction
though not as extensively as from The Grapes of Wrath.
Generally, what has been said here about Steinbeck's practice of excerpting from his 1939 novel also applies to these
other works.[115]

Chapter Four

UNCOLLECTED STORIES OF THE
1940s AND 1950s

Introduction

Although Steinbeck's best-known short fiction appears
in The Long Valley, this collection by no means marks the
end of his career as a story writer. During the 1940s and
50s Steinbeck continued to write and sell short pieces to
such popular magazines as Colliers, Harper's, Playboy, Reader's Digest, Punch, and the Atlantic.[1] These later stories--
including two O. Henry Award winners--were never published
in a collected edition and with a few exceptions have been
forgotten. Steinbeck's work from this period differs from
his Long Valley tales in several ways: while nearly every
story of the 1930s, as we have seen, reveals the author's
identification with that region in California known as "Steinbeck Country," settings in the later works become more national and international in scope. Steinbeck takes us abroad
to England, Northern Africa, Mexico, France, and then home
again to the America of his youth (California) and of his later
years (New York).

The frequently urban settings of these later stories
radically change the atmosphere of Steinbeck's fiction: as a
close observer of nature in The Long Valley, he draws crisp
images of the floral and animal life around the Salinas Valley;
in his uncollected tales of the 1940s and 50s, however, he
often turns indoors to domestic scenes, sometimes modeling
characters after members of his own immediate family. Noticeably absent are such "strong women" as Elisa Allen in
"The Chrysanthemums" (1937) and such animal-like and grotesque creatures as "Johnny Bear" (1937). Beginning in the
late 1940s, stories became increasingly autobiographical. In

tales like "His Father" (1949), Steinbeck paints thinly veiled
protraits of himself: an urban, middle-class family man (or
divorced father) preoccupied with the concerns of his children.

Besides Steinbeck's tendency to use himself and his
family as characters, another striking feature of these later
stories is their diversity in style: loose and episodic ("The
Summer Before" [1955]), tight, spare, and objective ("How
Mr. Hogan Robbed a Bank" [1956]), allegorical ("The Short-
Short Story of Mankind" [1955]), as well as the elevated,
Poesque style of "Affair at 7, Rue de M---" (1955).   Steinbeck also introduces several new themes including divorce,
nuclear holocaust, and a child's discovery of sexual differences.   At the same time, he continues to develop familiar
themes of the 30s, such as "respectability" as in his first
story published during the 1940s, "How Edith McGillcuddy
Met R.L. Stevenson."

"How Edith McGillcuddy Met R.L. Stevenson"
(1941)

Although the story was published in August, 1941,
Steinbeck composed the O. Henry Memorial Award winning
"How Edith McGillcuddy Met R.L. Stevenson" seven years
earlier in 1934.[2]   With its careful descriptions of flowers,
birds, and animals of the Salinas Valley, "Edith McGillcuddy"
reminds one of "The White Quail" (1935) and "The Chrysanthemums" (1937), both written during the same period.   The
narrative, based on a true incident told to Steinbeck by Mrs.
Edith Wagner, begins one Sunday morning in Salinas during
the summer of 1879.   Twelve-year-old Edith ambles innocently toward Sunday school when she is enticed by the bare-
footed Suzy Nugger to ride a funeral train to Monterey.   Once
at the cemetery, Edith wanders to the seashore and stumbles
upon a frowzy little girl named Lizzie, who leads her to an
unusual couple: a woman who smokes cigarettes and a long-
haired man.   Lizzie disappears, leaving Edith behind to enjoy tea with her congenial hosts.   When the whistle of the
returning funeral train blows, Edith scurries away, and the
tale ends: "that was how Edith McGillcuddy met Robert
Louis Stevenson."[3]

While the ostensible point of Edith's journey is her

chance meeting with the Scottish writer,[4] Steinbeck focuses
greater attention on her position in the moral and social
hierarchy of frontier Salinas. According to Steinbeck, in
1879 the "dirty little California cow-town" of Salinas con-
sisted of three moral elements: the "vicious," the "wavering," and the "good." Although the McGillcuddys are a
pious family who belong to the "good" element, Edith occasionally drifts toward the "vicious" "in the manner of the
company she [keeps]" (p. 559). Steinbeck's three-part di-
vision of the community is particularly evident on the funeral
train. Passengers riding in the front cars belong to the
"good" people of Salinas: "ladies and gentlemen in black
formal clothes [sitting] stiffly" (p. 562), along with the of-
ficiating priest. These are the town's stern and righteous
citizens. Cars further back carry Salinas' "wavering"
populace--"less formal" riders crowding together with their
"lunch baskets and paper bags and cans of milk" cluttered
between the seats (p. 563). Upon seeing this middle group,
Edith sighs with relief that she and Suzy are "not the only
ones who were combining a funeral and a free train ride"
(p. 563). The "vicious" layer--frequenters of the town's
twenty saloons, as well as Suzy Nugger and her ilk--ride in
the last car, where several boys are fighting, snatching the
caps of passengers, and throwing them from the speeding
train. Thus, Steinbeck seats passengers according to their
social position in the community. The nearer to the front of
the train, the closer they are to the priest and the "good"
element--and hence to "respectability."

But even as Steinbeck divides the train's passengers
into a social hierarchy, he begins to blur these distinctions
with colorful floral and animal imagery. As the train puffs
away from the station, its bell tolling mournfully, wind rushes
by, blowing flowers and ruffling women's dresses and the
priest's surplice. In the stir created by the departing train,
sparrows and blackbirds take to wing, ladies push back their
veils to gobble sandwiches, and children throw "orange peels
and apple cores at one another" (p. 564). The birds, veiled
women, ruffled priest, and frolicking children all embraced
by the flower-perfumed breeze emphasize the oneness of all
things. Even the locomotive becomes a part of this indivisible whole, personified as an iron horse with head of billow-
ing black smoke, and belly puffing clouds of vapor. Steinbeck seems to suggest that, moral and social hierarchy not-
withstanding, all passengers ride on the same train to the
same destination.

Even though the various layers of Salinas life commingle
on the funeral train, none of its passengers can shift from
one element to another as does Edith. Once she leaves home
neatly dressed for Sunday school, Edith's deteriorating appearance reflects her fall from the best level of Salinas society to the worst: when she climbs aboard the train with
Suzy, Edith's "stiff and perfect" pink hair ribbon--signifying
the "good" element--is ruined (p. 560); she scuffs her brightly polished shoes; her face becomes "streaked with red" (p.
563) from an all-day sucker Suzy gives her. And finally,
Edith tears the knee out of one of her stockings (p. 563).
By the time Edith's journey is complete, she resembles a
waif like her low-life companions, Suzy and Lizzie.

In this soiled and disheveled condition, Edith meets
Robert Louis Stevenson--the "long-haired young man" whose
eyes are "shining with fever" (p. 570). Stevenson's sickly
appearance, according to Roy S. Simmonds, can be attributed
to "almost a month of hardship spent crossing the Atlantic
and the North American continent" to be reunited with his
beloved, Fanny Osborne.[5] Edith's brief encounter with
Stevenson and his companion--while no doubt the origin of
Steinbeck's interest in the tale--fills only a small part of the
narrative. Steinbeck devotes the larger portion to the theme
of dubious "respectability," showing how the daughter of a
"good" Salinas family, in order to meet the renowned author,
must be lured from her righteous (if somewhat hesitant) path
toward Sunday school by the "wavering" and "vicious" elements of this burgeoning frontier town. "How Edith McGillcuddy Met R.L. Stevenson" is perhaps the most poetically
sensitive story Steinbeck published during the 1940s and 50s.
While a masterpiece in subtlety and tone, the story also demonstrates some of Steinbeck's most effective--because nearly
imperceptible--social criticism.

Wartime Stories
(1943)

One bibliographical challenge in the study of Steinbeck's short fiction of this period involves the author's New
York Herald Tribune dispatches from the European theatre
during World War II. As we can observe from the selection
of these in Once There Was a War (1958), Steinbeck the
journalist is often indistinguishable from Steinbeck the fiction

writer. Is "Craps," for example, an impressionistic account
of an actual event?[6] Is it fictionalized, and therefore a
short story? Or is it a little of both? Some pieces in Once
There Was a War, like "Bob Hope" (pp. 88–91) and "Lilli
Marlene" (pp. 62–65), cannot be mistaken for fiction, but
others like "Craps" certainly can.

     In the introduction to his 1958 volume, Steinbeck
says "[t]he events set down here did happen" (p. xi).
Yet in the same breath he confesses that some of the pieces
are "fairy tales.... They are as real as the wicked witch
and the good fairy, as true and tested and edited as any
other myth" (pp. xx-xxi). Moreover, Steinbeck closes the
introduction as if he were launching into a fictional narrative:
"[t]here was a war, long ago--once upon a time" (p. xxi).
Most critics agree that at least some of the dispatches in
Once There Was a War are fictional. Warren French remarks
that "some of the reports ... have an embryonic fictional
form." Similarly, Peter Lisca says, "occasionally, the com-
muniques are in the form of short stories...."[7]

     Steinbeck often attributes his war "stories" to someone
other than himself. He begins "Craps," for example, by
calling it "one of Mulligan's lies" (p. 112). Similarly, in
"The Cottage That Wasn't There" (p. 68), he introduces an
Army sergeant to narrate the tale. Steinbeck very seldom
takes responsibility for what he says in Once There Was
a War: "I never admitted having seen anything myself.
In describing a scene I invariably put it in the mouth of
someone else" (p. xvi). Consequently, the reader is hard-
pressed to find a single "I" in the entire volume. On those
infrequent occasions when Steinbeck refers to himself, he
does so obliquely by saying, "this writer" (p. 102).

     By doing this, Steinbeck distances himself from his
subjects, who are predominantly quick-witted enlisted men
like Private Big Train Mulligan (pp. 84, 102), Eddie the crapshooter (p. 112), and Sligo the clever deserter (p. 130). In
other words, Steinbeck covers the "human interest" stories--
"the hopes, fears, and activities of 'G.I. Joes' under the
various conditions of war."[8] Occasionally he focuses on the
few lieutenants and captains among the men; but for the most
part his heart belongs to the little guys who fight for their
country and their lives, without much say in how the battle
lines are drawn. The protagonists in Once There Was a War,

then, are like the Joads in <u>The Grapes of Wrath</u> (1939):
common people caught up in forces beyond their control, yet
usually with the will and cleverness enough to endure.

One dispatch in which Steinbeck obviously colors facts
with fancy is "The Story of an Elf" (pp. 190-94), first reprinted in 1944 as "The Elf in Algiers."[9] The story takes
place in the Alletti Hotel in Algiers amidst a gathering of
thirsty war correspondents and a British consul. Suddenly
in a puff of blue smoke, a small elf appears. The leprechaun
introduces himself as "Charlie Lytle," a self-appointed provider
of happiness for weary troops and journalists. At the request
of one reporter, the elf causes three cases of Haig and Haig
scotch to materialize out of nowhere. The delighted men call
it a miracle. But one of them, Jack Belden, is unconvinced.
He asks for a bottle of "La Blatt's Pale India Ale," and instantly Charlie Lytle produces it. That night the euphoric
correspondents find that they even enjoy an air raid.

"The Story of an Elf," is obviously one of the "fairy
tales" Steinbeck refers to in his introduction to <u>Once There
Was a War</u> (p. xx). That the piece is fabricated from his
own imagination is evidenced by Steinbeck's long-standing
interest in leprechauns. When a student at Stanford, Steinbeck often told stories to his friends about ghosts and elves.
One such story, recalls Stanford classmate Frank Fenton, involved a "blue leprechaun who flung a ham on the floor...."
Steinbeck, says Fenton, "insisted that leprechauns and elves
were very real...."[10] The similarities between this early elf
story and the later one appearing in <u>Once There Was a War</u>
are too obvious to mention. Steinbeck had apparently managed to keep alive his fascination with leprechauns even
through the war.

One example of a dispatch that Steinbeck puts "in the
mouth of someone else" (p. xvi) is "The Cottage That Wasn't
There" (pp. 68-71). The narrative opens in London near
Hyde Park's lake Serpentine, where a sergeant lying in the
grass begins to narrate what he calls a "ghost story" (pp. 68-
69). The sergeant explains that one night when walking along
a country raod, he saw a light shining in the window of a
cottage. Inside the scene was pleasant: a small fireplace, a
white cat, and a woman, about fifty, sewing. The sergeant
was puzzled that the cottage had no blackout curtains, yet he
decided not to question its inhabitants. Even more puzzling,

however, was the soldier's later recollection that there is no
cottage on that country road, only the bombed-out remains of
one. This worries him because, as he tells us, he doesn't
"'believe stuff like that'" (p. 71). In "The Cottage That Wasn't
There" Steinbeck cannot be accused of telling half-truths or
lies, because evidently he records the sergeant's tale exactly
as he heard it. Nevertheless, the resulting narrative has all
the earmarks of a short story, including an O. Henry surprise ending. True facts seldom arrange themselves in such
tight dramatic form. Yet, similar surprise endings occur in
other stories Steinbeck borrows from talkative G.I.s.

Such a tale is "Craps" (pp. 112-116). That Steinbeck
repeats this story second-hand has already been established:
"This is one of Mulligan's lies ..." (p. 112), he confesses.
"Mulligan" is "Private Big Train Mulligan" (pp. 84, 102), the
subject of two earlier dispatches in Once There Was a War.
"Craps" features a wizard crapshooter named Eddie who never
loses on Sunday. Several crap games spring up when Eddie's
troop ship sails on Tuesday, but he resists them until Sunday.
when stakes become higher and he knows he can win. He
walks into the hottest game on deck and begins to win big.
Suspense builds as he rolls for the largest pot of the day.
Snake eyes! Eddie loses. In disbelief, he gasps, "'I win on
Sunday, always win on Sunday'" (p. 116). Then a sergeant
explains that before Eddie's fateful roll, the ship had crossed
the international date line and, by doing so, Sunday was lost.
This unexpected conclusion suggests that, rather than merely
a factual dispatch, "Craps" is a consciously-crafted narrative.

Given the example of "Craps" and the other wartime
stories discussed above, how are we to evaluate Steinbeck's
insistant remark: "The events set down here
did happen" (p. xi)?   We can certainly believe Steinbeck's claim that someone (such as a puzzled sergeant or a
Private Big Train Mulligan) told him these stories. Yet does
this mean that the events depicted actually took place?
Steinbeck's cautionary words provide the most reliable answer:
these pieces are "as real as the wicked witch and the good
fairy, as true and tested and edited as any other myth" (p.
xxi).

"The Time the Wolves Ate the Vice-Principal"
(1947)

Four years after filing his sometimes fanciful dispatches
from the war, Steinbeck published a shockingly different kind
of story in the obscure '47, Magazine of the Year. "The Time
the Wolves Ate the Vice-Principal" (March, 1947) is a rejected
interchapter from Cannery Row (1945) which, according to
Peter Lisca, Steinbeck's publishers concluded bore "little relationship to the rest of the book."[11] In addition to its
gruesome violence, the tale's Salinas backdrop makes it un-
fit for Steinbeck's novel set among the sardine canneries of
Monterey.

Written in the objective, spare style of "Flight" (1938),
"The Time The Wolves Ate the Vice-Principal" describes the
grisly slaughter of Mr. Hartley, an ailing high school admin-
istrator. Early one morning a pack of wolves gathers on the
lawn of the Salinas courthouse. One great gray wolf leads
them through the streets to an old Airedale, which they instantly devour. Next they come upon Mr. Loman, who is
opening his music store. Fortunately, Loman spots them and
quickly slams the door. Finally, the wolves pick up the
scent of Mr. Hartley. Although Hartley sees them coming a
block away, his flight is in vain. The wolves catch him on
Mrs. Harris's porch and rip him to pieces. The sleeping
Mrs. Harris doesn't even wake up.

"The Time the Wolves Ate the Vice-Principal" provides
yet another example of Steinbeck's "Phalanx" theory, showing
how several stray animals, given a leader, can be transformed
into a ravenous "gray mass."[12] They sniff aimlessly on the
courthouse lawn until the great gray wolf appears and then
"a kind of purpose" comes on them (p. 26). The story also
demonstrates Steinbeck's ability to shape even the sparest
materials into a naturalistic drama. Clearly, in this tale only
the fittest survive. Of the wolves' intended victims, two are
aged and infirm, and cannot defend themselves. The Airedale is "dignified," but "so old he did not smell [the wolves]
coming" (p. 26). The convalescing vice-principal, Mr. Hartley, runs too slowly to escape them. Only the "fit" character
--the sharp-eyed and quick Mr. Logan--survives.

Beyond these Phalanx and Darwinian themes, Warren
French suggests that in "Wolves" Steinbeck attacks "respect-

able" society's insensitivity and moral indifference. That
Mrs. Harris slumbers through the vice-principal's slaughter
is an example of this dangerous complacency. According to
French, Steinbeck believed that such lax attitudes helped to
facilitate World War II, a war he had just witnessed on several fronts before he wrote this gruesome tale.[13] Given its
compactness and unity of effect, "The Time the Wolves Ate
the Vice-Principal" is a satisfying tale. Its coldly objective
description of Mr. Hartley's slaughter reminds one of Steinbeck's unsentimental account of propagating and expiring
tidepool animals in The Sea of Cortez (1941).

The Josh Billings Story
and other Intercalary Chapters
in Cannery Row (1945)

While "The Time the Wolves Ate the Vice-Principal" is
the only Cannery Row interchapter (although omitted) to have
been published separately, several other of these interpolated
tales can be read independently of the novel. Peter Lisca
identifies nine such interchapters which "are entirely self-
contained."[14] The most self-contained of all is a tale whose
plot and characters seem very remote from the main narrative, and whose date of composition precedes by several
years that of Cannery Row. On February 12, 1939 Steinbeck wrote to Elizabeth Otis: "The Josh Billings story I
just haven't written. The leg has been too bad."[15] The
"Josh Billings story" Steinbeck refers to is the offbeat piece
published six years later in Cannery Row. Appearing as
Chapter Twelve in the novel, this sketch chronicles the
meandering journey of the famous humorist's intestines,
haphazardly discarded by an embalmer after Billings' death
and only at the last minute rescued from becoming mackerel
bait.

Although critics have postulated thematic similarities
between the Josh Billings tale and surrounding chapters in
Cannery Row, this interchapter is an odd addition to the
novel. Peter Lisca calls the Billings piece one of the few
interchapters "whose function is obscure." Lisca conjec-
tures that the tale is perhaps "only intended to illustrate
the great difference between the public's slight regard for
a living literary figure and its disproportionate concern for
the disposition of his dead body."[16] Similarly, Warren

French admits that the Billings "episode does not at first
seem related to the preceding chapter [eleven] about the
Palace Flophouse boys' difficulties in fixing a truck that
they borrowed for a frog hunt." French suggests that both
of these chapters burlesque people's "suspicions of innovations that will ultimately change their culture," innovations
like the Model T Ford (appearing in Chapter Eleven) and the
embalming of a corpse before interment (alluded to in Chapter Twelve).[17] If these justifications for inclusion of the
Billings piece seem far-fetched, it may be because Steinbeck
did not compose the odd narrative specifically for Cannery
Row. Moreover, Billings died in 1885, some fifty years before the action in the novel takes place.

    Another interchapter like the Josh Billings tale which
stands out from the main plot is Chapter Twenty-four, the
story of an aspiring but broke writer/cartoonist and his
imaginative wife. The Tom and Mary Talbot story is unique
for two reasons: first, at about 1,200 words, it is twice as
long as the average interchapter in Cannery Row. And,
second, it lacks the waterfront setting of most of the novel's
episodes. It may be assumed that, because of its context,
the piece transpires somewhere near Cannery Row; however,
nothing in the sketch suggests this. The backdrop might
just as likely be Salinas, where fantasy-prone Mary Teller
in "The White Quail" talks to her flowers in much the same
way that Mary Talbot visits with her neighborhood cats.

    Outside of the Josh Billings tale and perhaps the Tom
and Mary Talbot narrative, the balance of the Cannery Row
interchapters seem to have been composed specifically for
the novel. Of these, a few generalities can be made: most
are approximately 600 words in length and present a cameo
of a single character or a pair of characters. Only one interchapter departs from this pattern: Chapter Two, in which
Steinbeck establishes an atmosphere--or better, a perspective
--through which the reader may view the entire novel. But
after Chapter Two, the remaining interchapters focus on
such characters as the old Chinaman with the flapping shoe
sole (Ch. 4); Mr. and Mrs. Malloy, who live in a rusting
boiler pipe (Ch. 8); the uncoordinated and unloved Frankie
(Ch. 10); the skater atop Holman's flagpole, and the curiosity he arouses (Ch. 19); Henri the painter (Ch. 22); Joey
and Willard's disagreement and fight (Ch. 24); Frankie's
theft of a clock (Ch. 28); and the lonely gopher in search
of a mate (Ch. 31).

"The Miracle of Tepayac"
(1948)

Published on Christmas day, 1948, in Colliers, "The
Miracle of Tepayac" marks a radical departure from the re-
ligiously unorthodox Cannery Row. Drawing on the Our
Lady of Guadalupe legend of 1531, Steinbeck retells the
story of Juan Diego, an Indian widower who wanders in the
mountains near Cuautitlan, Mexico. One morning upon reaching the summit of Tepayac, Juan Diego experiences a vision
of the Queen of Heaven, who orders him to have the Bishop
of Mexico erect a temple in her honor on Tepayac. When
Juan Diego visits Mexico City, however, the Bishop tells him
to reflect upon the vision and come back later. Then the
Indian hikes once more up Tepayac, where the Holy Mother
encourages him to seek out the bishop again. But, as before, the bishop sends him away, this time to bring from the
Virgin a "sign beyond words."[18] Finally she does provide
Juan Diego such a sign: beautiful roses of Castile which
Juan Diego gathers into his cloak. When the Indian delivers
them to the Bishop, the roses have imprinted the image of
the Virgin on the cactus-fiber cloak. Falling to his knees,
the bishop agrees to build a temple to Our Lady of Guadalupe on Mount Tepayac, and the happy Juan Diego cares for
the shrine until his death.

The stark contrasts between the lofty heights of Tepayac where Juan Diego receives his vision and the world
below of Mexico City where the Bishop resides show Steinbeck in his familiar role of advocate for the common man.
During Juan Diego's shuttles between these two locales, the
mount of Tepayac becomes a kind of "church invisible" where
Juan Diego's soul is filled with the spiritual presence of the
Virgin. The Bishop's chamber, on the other hand, is to the
Indian merely the "church visible," where the prelate carries
on the administrative functions of worship, but without di-
rect communication with the Holy Mother. Because the Lady
selects the humble Juan Diego to deliver her sign, the roles
of priest and parishioner are reversed: the common man's
vision takes precedence over the prelate's ecclesiastical authority.

The story of Our Lady of Guadalupe has been retold
many times since its legendary occurrence on Saturday, December 9, 1531. Willa Cather, for example, recounts it in
her novel, Death Comes For the Archbishop (1927). Steinbeck's

version of the tale is interesting for its attributing grief to
Juan Diego over the loss of his wife, Maria Lucia. Steinbeck
seems to diverge from the legend when he says that at the
time the Virgin appeared to Juan Diego on Tepayac he was
"lost in sorrow" (p. 22). According to the legend, Maria
Lucia had died in 1529, two years before her husband saw
his vision. Rather than "wandering over the hills, spending
his strength the way a grieving man does" (p. 22) as Steinbeck characterizes the Indian, Juan Diego was merely hiking
to mass over the mountain as he and Maria Lucia had done
every Saturday morning for many years.[19] This slight departure from established sources has autobiographical implications: having recently lost his second wife through divorce
in October, 1948, and his friend, Ed Ricketts, to a train accident a few months earlier, Steinbeck himself may have felt
the pain he attributes to Juan Diego in "The Miracle."

        That Steinbeck needed to write to take his mind off his
suffering, and perhaps even to make money after a financially
upsetting divorce, is evidenced in "Miracle." While he adds
a few personal touches to the legend, it lacks the vigor,
earthiness, and rich imagery of his best short fiction. Later
in his life, Steinbeck's creative abilities would revive and he
would write one of the finest short stories of his career.
Presently, however, he seemed to be impaired by the tragic
events of the year.

                            "His Father"
                             (1949)

        While we must read between the lines in "The Miracle
of Tepayac" to find evidence of Steinbeck's troubled personal
life during the late 1940s, in the autobiographical "His Father," he deals directly with one of his gravest concerns:
separation from his two sons. With the breakup of Steinbeck's marriage to Gwyndolyn Conger, his two boys were to
live with their mother in New York. According to the divorce settlement, Steinbeck (then residing in Pacific Grove,
California) would have them for two months during each summer. The first of these annual visits was to take place in
the summer of 1949. But even before then, Steinbeck became eager to see his sons. Traveling on impulse to New
York sometime in April, he became concerned after seeing
that his children had as their only playground a busy urban

street.[20] Upon returning to California, Steinbeck wrote a
brief short story based on this reunion with his boys, which
appeared the following September in Reader's Digest.[21]

"His Father," filling only two-and-a-half pages of the
magazine, concerns a young boy taunted by insensitive children about his missing father. Once the children learn that
the boy's parents are divorced, they glare at him with accus-
ing eyes. Distraught and angry, he nonetheless endures
their abuse until one day his father unexpectedly appears.
To his playmates, the happy boy exclaims, "'He's here!
You want to see him?'" (p. 21).

The fictional father who surprises his son with an un-
announced visit is obviously modeled after Steinbeck himself.
"His Father" is autobiographical in other ways as well. The
protagonist, "going on seven years old," resembles Steinbeck's first son, Thom, who was five when the story appeared. The urban setting with "taxis and kids and tricy-
cles and baby buggies" suggests the neighborhood in New
York where the two boys lived with their mother. And the
atmosphere of suffering which imbues this city-scape is evidently a reflection of young Thom Steinbeck's (and perhaps
the author's) despondency (p. 19).

For such a brief story, "His Father" is built upon a
rather intricate chronology. Most essential background information is narrated through flashbacks, especially the
young protagonist's painful encounters with his neighbors.
These flashbacks set the stage in the last scene for the father's unexpected visit. Thus, the story develops and maintains psychological tension which is not relieved until the
closing lines. Besides its noteworthy focus on a topical
subject--the children of divorce--"His Father" marks the
first time Steinbeck uses himself and his family as models
for characters in his fiction.

"The Great Roque War"
and
"The Pacific Grove Butterfly Festival"
in Sweet Thursday (1954)

Like The Grapes of Wrath and Cannery Row, Sweet
Thursday is another Steinbeck novel in which intercalary

chapters appear. In this 1954 volume, however, only Chapter 8, "The Great Roque War" and Chapter 38, "Hooptedoodle
(2), or The Pacific Grove Butterfly Festival" are autonomous
stories. Coincidentally, both of these concern the town of
Pacific Grove, California.

In "The Great Roque War" Steinbeck focuses on the
obsession of Pacific Grove residents over a complicated version of croquet. Originally intended for leisure and recrea-
tion, the roque courts quickly become a literal battle ground
because of fierce competition between "the Greens" and its
opposition, "the Blues." The bitter rivalry begins to pene-
trate all aspects of life, including politics. Finally, Deems,
the man who donated the courts to the town, hires a bull-
dozer to turn them into a "ragged hole in the ground."[22]
This proves to be the only way to check the roque epidemic.

Pacific Grove citizens look equally bad in "Hooptedoodle
(2)," which concerns their annual Monarch butterfly festival.
Through some quirk of nature "great clouds of orangy Monarch butterflies" (p. 259) return at the same time every year
to Pacific Grove. Once their migration begins to attract
tourists, the town fathers--equating tourism with dollars--
decide to cash in on this natural wonder. They create the
"Great Butterfly Festival," which brings the city profits until one fateful year when the Monarchs do not return. Sin
is blamed, as the community goes into convulsions over their
lost revenue and credibility.

Both of these Sweet Thursday interchapters are ironic
and mildly humorous; yet neither furthers the main plot concerning the romance of Doc and Suzy. Though we might
grant that these two interchapters add a certain tone or atmosphere, both are essentially isolated from the rest of the
novel in terms of plot and character. They also indicate a
gradual shift in the subject matter of Steinbeck's short fiction from serious domestic issues in "His Father" to the humorous, even bizarre episode discussed next in "The Affair
at 7, Rue de M---."

"Affair at 7, Rue de M---"

(1955)

Readers familiar with The Short Reign of Pippin IV

(1957) will recognize the Paris setting of Steinbeck's second
O. Henry Award-winning story from this period, "The Affair
at 7, Rue de M---." Its subject matter, style, and tone,
however, are worlds apart from anything Steinbeck had previously written. At this phase in his career, Steinbeck seems
to have experienced a crisis in style, fearing that his emi-
nently successful techniques of the 1930s were becoming a
kind of "straitjacket," threatening to destroy him as a writer.[23] Hence, he tried to set out in a new direction: "A
whole revolution is going on in me," he told Elia Kazan.
"It's hard to throw over 30 years work but necessary if the
work has pooped out. It isn't that it was bad but that I've
used it up."[24]

Steinbeck's grappling for creative alternatives to his
earlier style is evident in the exaggerated Poesque atmosphere
of "Affair at 7, Rue de M---," which blends gothic elements
with the detached tone of a detective story. The plot is
simple, yet extraordinary: To an old, distinguished address
in Paris, an American writer brings his wife, daughter, and
two little sons. John, the younger son, enjoys chewing bub-
ble gum until one day he discovers his gum is chewing itself! John's father extracts the moist blob from the boy's
mouth and places it on a desk, but the gum--still pulsating
--slides back toward the boy. The father hurls it out the
window, but the gum returns. Then he beats it with an
African war club and drops it into the Seine. That night
the gum returns. Finally, he covers the undulating blob
with a bell jar. After one week, the once menacing gum
finally becomes languid, no longer a threat to young John.

Right from the story's title, "Affair at 7, Rue de M---"
Steinbeck seems to parody Edgar Allan Poe. We might recall
"The Murders in the Rue Morgue" (1841), for example, also
set in Paris and whose tragic events are even referred to in
the tale as an "affair." And Steinbeck's cool and rational
first-person narrator (modeled after Steinbeck himself) resembles Poe's meerschaum-puffing raconteur in "Rue Morgue."
It is perhaps no coincidence, then, that Steinbeck's narrator
lights his own pipe at the close of "Affair at 7, Rue de
M---."

Other Poesque touches include the "African war club
... studded with brass" with which young John's father
beats the renegade gum into a thin pulp,[25] and an ornate,

elevated style in which Steinbeck's customary Anglo-Saxon
diction gives way to Romance and Latinate parlance like
"arrondissement" and "aficionado" (pp. 258, 259). For example, the eight-year-old John says to his father, "'I came to
your work room to await your first disengagement, wishing to
acquaint you with my difficulty'" (p. 261). One would be hard-
pressed to find such a stilted expression in Steinbeck's earlier work, especially spoken by a child. Obviously, Steinbeck wrote "Affair" with French readers (whose fancy for
Poe is well known) in mind. The story appeared first in
French--as "L' Affaire du l' avenue de M---" (Figaro, 436
[August 28, 1954] I)--and not until nearly one year later in
English, in Haper's Bazaar. With its oddly humorous subject
and elevated diction, "Affair at 7, Rue de M---" is an un-
characteristic Steinbeck story which demonstrates the author's
versatility and willingness to experiment.

"The Summer Before"
(1955)

Published in the British magazine Punch and (unlike
"Affair") never reprinted in America, "The Summer Before"
(May, 1955) provides a warm glimpse of Steinbeck's early
days in Salinas. The story includes a humorous sketch of
the author's childhood pony, Jill, and cameo appearances by
his sister, Mary, and his young friends, Glen Graves and
Max Wagner. With its Salinas backdrop, child characters,
and loose, episodic construction, "The Summer Before" resembles The Red Pony, except that in "Summer" Steinbeck
adopts the first-person point of view. The main plot involves
Willie Morton, a Salinas boy who lives with his protective
mother. One summer day Willie's friends invite him to a
swimming party on the Salinas River, but his mother screams
in opposition. Willie ultimately defies her and joins his friends
on the river bank. When they strip off their clothes to swim,
however, Willie refuses to disrobe. Later, his friends return
from the water to discover Willie missing. Soon they spot him
under water caught by his overalls' strap on a sunken tree.
When a nearby Japanese farmer rescues him, Willie's strap
breaks and his pants fall down. To everyone's amazement,
Willie is a girl!

Steinbeck plants several clues in the narrative about
Willie's gender. The other boys know Willie is somewhat

"strange just by the way he [stands] off and [looks]" at
them.[26] In addition, Willie's mother carefully insures that
Willie uses the toilet alone and avoids swimming with the
neighborhood boys (pp. 649, 651). Despite these hints, the
story's ending still surprises. And no one is more surprised
than Willie's friends--several boys intrigued by their inadver-
tent discovery about Willie. Yet, in "The Summer Before,"
Steinbeck seems little inclined to explore the implications of
their new sexual knowledge, and instead uses the narrative
as an occasion to string together several loose strands of his
childhood memories of Salinas. The first third of the narrative, in fact, contains several reminiscences unrelated to the
story's central action. Due to these autobiographical indul-
gences, the story lacks structural unity. Nonetheless, Steinbeck's charming vignettes about his pony and childhood
friends offer readers a rare look at the author's early years
through his own eyes.

"The Short-Short Story of Mankind"
(or "We're Holding Our Own")[27]
(1955)

While "The Summer Before" demonstrates that Steinbeck was able to recall events nearly fifty years in his past,
in "The Short-Short Story of Mankind" he turns to his present day (the 1950s) for material, focusing on a crucial issue
of the day: nuclear war. His method of dealing with this
topical subject, however, is to envision the origins of war in
prehistoric times. Steinbeck chronicles a series of quarrels
that break out among different tribes, beginning in the stone
age. In this brief allegory, he shows how innovative people
whose inventions stand to benefit mankind are slain by their
jealous and ignorant contemporaries--"Nobody can put a knife
in the status quo and get away with it" (p. 328). Stone
age Elmer, for example, invents a rock and brush house and
is slain for his efforts. Ironically, Elmer's own people later
embrace his invention and worship him as a deity. Then
Max designs a tent of animal skin and suffers the same fate
as did Elmer. Violence among tribes and against individuals
continues until modern times. Then missiles render geographic
boundaries irrelevant, and nations begin to merge. Concludes
the narrator, we have no other choice: join together or face
extinction.

When "The Short-Short Story of Mankind" first appeared
in November, 1955, the threat of nuclear war, and hence of
human extinction, loomed ominously on the horizon.[28] Steinbeck apparently wrote the story to conjecture about the pos-
sibilities for survival of the human race, noting our tendency
to resist change, and to destroy those who perpetrate it.
These twin tendencies do not bode well for mankind; for how
can a people progress if they systematically eliminate those
who would lead them out of the darkness? The irony of this
is not lost on Steinbeck, who sees the same kind of behavior
mirrored in modern times: "Now we've got the United Nations
and the elders are right in there fighting it the way they
fought coming out of caves" (p. 329). Today, as in the
past, the old and conventional thwart the young and inven-
tive. Steinbeck concludes that we must change our ways,
for "It'd be kind of silly if we killed ourselves off after all
this time" (p. 329).

The charge by some critics that Steinbeck's later works
suffer from excessive moralizing seems warranted with regard
to "The Short-Short Story of Mankind." Only one-fourth of
the piece contains dialogue, while the bulk comprises an obvious allegory in which Steinbeck tells (rather than shows)
the reader what is wrong with the human race. Considering
the complexities involved, his prescription to cure our collec-
tive ills seems simplistic. Moreover, the story's alternating
humorous and pessimistic tone blurs whatever statement Steinbeck had intended to make.

"How Mr. Hogan Robbed a Bank"
(1956)

Just four months after "The Short-Short Story of Mankind" appeared, Steinbeck's most artistically successful story
of the 1940s and 50s was published in the Atlantic Monthly.
The setting and central characters of "How Mr. Hogan Robbed
a Bank" are familiar to readers of Winter of Our Discontent
(1961), yet the story's theme is markedly different from that
of the novel. While Ethan Allen Hawley in Winter fully under-
stands the moral implications of succumbing to the temptations
of pride, greed, and betrayal of friends and associates, Mr.
Hogan's bank robbery affords him not the slightest pang of
guilt. Steinbeck gives no indication of Hogan's motives, and
refuses to attribute any larger meaning to his actions.[29]

Since Mr. Hogan--a grocery clerk, husband, and father
--realizes that most bank robberies fail from excessive "hanky-
panky," he keeps his theft simple. For one year he observes
activity at the bank around the corner from the grocery store
where he works. Early on the day of the heist, a Saturday
morning before Labor Day, Hogan walks to the grocery store,
cuts out a Mickey Mouse mask from a cereal box, and grabs
a silver revolver. Entering the bank just after it opens, he
steals more than eight thousand dollars and flees. That evening he hides the cash in a case holding his Knight's Templar
uniform, except for two five-dollar bills: one he gives to his
son for receiving honorable mention in an "I Love America"
essay contest, and the other to his daughter for being a good
sport. "'What a fine family!'" Mr. Hogan concludes. "'Fine!'"[30]

Warren French has called "Mr. Hogan" "truly vintage
Steinbeck," a story in which he finally "achieves the non-
teleological viewpoint he [had] long sought."[31] All indica-
tions suggest, however, that when he wrote the story Steinbeck had none of these aspirations in mind. As frequently
happened in his career, some works he expected to be "major"
became critical failures, while others which he wrote merely
for his own relaxation were highly acclaimed. Examples of
this latter type include "The Gift" and Cannery Row. To
these two works, "Mr. Hogan" may be added. Steinbeck expressed wonderment at the circumstances of its composition:

> I am constantly amazed and to a certain extent
> frightened by the vagrant tendency of my mind and
> writing direction. It seems so often to take its own
> direction--can be resisted but goes into a pout if it
> is resisted. An example of this was "Mr. Hogan."
> I had no intention of writing him. He just started
> and came out.[32]

Consequently, "Mr. Hogan" appeared as a lighthearted,
"frivolous satire and fantasy,"[33] a "smart-alec work ... rare
among Steinbeck's" works.[34] Unlike the typical crime or detective story, it offers few surprises and generates little, if
any, suspense. Nothing about Hogan's bank heist is nerve-
racking, breathtaking, or even mildly exciting. Steinbeck
describes the robbery in such matter-of-fact terms that grand
theft begins to resemble any mundane routine like making tea.
Yet while routines often become mindless, Mr. Hogan's caper
is a thoroughly conceived and highly conscious act. Steinbeck

underscores this contrast between Hogan's way of doing
things and that of his peers (who do not "notice things" as
he does) and satirizes the "dangers of getting into a rut"--
of becoming so stultified by habit as to lose the capacity to
observe new and changing phenomena.[35] This is obviously
the plight of Hogan's friends and neighbors. The only real
surprise about his bank robbery is, then, that Hogan can so
easily outwit those around him whose lives are bound up in
leaden routines. Steinbeck implies that the superior person
is not so much the individual who behaves according to traditional values (e.g., the American work ethic) as the one who
is fully conscious and able to see through society's shams
and false bottoms. These are Mr. Hogan's strengths, and,
to paraphrase Steinbeck, they stand him in good stead.

"Case of the Hotel Ghost--Or ... What Are
You Smoking in That Pipe, Mr. S.?"
(or "Reunion at the Quiet Hotel")
(1957)

Though perhaps his finest story of the 1940s and 50s,
"How Mr. Hogan Robbed a Bank" was not to conclude Steinbeck's career in short fiction. "Case of the Hotel Ghost ..."
appeared on June 30, 1957 in the Louisville Courier-Journal;
an abbreviated version of the story (retitled "Reunion at the
Quiet Hotel") was published seven months later on January
25, 1958 in the London newspaper, the Evening Standard.
Both versions seem to be based on John and Elaine Steinbeck's experiences in Italy and England during a European
tour begun in March, 1952.[36]

The Courier-Journal text of the story begins with a
facetious comparison of Italian and English ghosts. Steinbeck mentions first a haunted house in Florence whose ap-
paritions frightened even the German occupation forces during the war. British ghosts, Steinbeck then implies, are
milder than their Italian counterparts. He reluctantly admits
having met the English variety once in London. The last
paragraph of this droll introduction in the Courier-Journal
text becomes the first paragraph of the Evening Standard
story. From this point on, the two narratives vary only
slightly from one another.

"Case of the Hotel Ghost--Or ... What Are You Smoking in That Pipe, Mr. S.?" involves the Steinbecks' brief

stay at a quiet London hotel where the author was quartered during the war. After Steinbeck's old cronies--Albert the desk clerk, Max the lift operator, and George the room attendant--greet him with indifferent politeness ("'It's just the English manner,'" Steinbeck tells his wife),[37] the couple retire to their room and dine on "thick, mushy soup completely without flavour" and "veal chops breaded with old washcloths" (p. 9). The next evening they decide to go out to an Armenian restaurant in Soho. Upon their return, the hotel has vanished. No trace of the building remains except a deep hole with rubble piled around it. Rather than try to explain the hotel's collapse, they merely inform the authorities that their passports have been stolen.

The crumbling hotel can be seen as a symbol for the narrator's abortive attempt to rekindle his memories of the war. That he can no longer find inspiration or solace in the past is perhaps an autobiographical statement. When the story appeared, Steinbeck was beginning to fear that he might never write well again. By 1960 Steinbeck reportedly had told Elizabeth Otis, "my time is over ... I should bow out."[38] "Case of the Hotel Ghost" may very well foreshadow the diminution of his powers, the collapsed building representing the last flickers of his creative light. The story, while engaging, lacks the vigor of Steinbeck's earlier work, its flaccid style echoing the theme of decay. Even though Steinbeck continued to write for nearly a decade more, his last known short story was to be this curious tale set on British soil and reprinted in the London Evening Standard in 1958.

CONCLUSION

In Beyond The Red Pony we have seen that Nobel laureate John Steinbeck wrote nearly fifty short stories, twice as many as are generally known today. In addition to his popular tales contained in The Pastures of Heaven (1932) and The Long Valley (1938), Steinbeck's canon includes close to twenty uncollected and unpublished pieces. When added to these are several intercalary chapters from his novels, as well as his many travel and wartime tales from his journalistic writings, Steinbeck's forgotten stories actually outnumber the familiar ones. This neglected half of his short fiction contains work of biographical and artistic importance, including two O. Henry Memorial Award winners.

Steinbeck began writing tales as an aspiring, but awkward apprentice in the 1920s, his work often imitating James Branch Cabell, Donn Byrne and other popular writers of the day. In the 1930s, Steinbeck emerged as a mature craftsman of short fiction, rediscovering the California people and places that would unleash his special genius. During this decade his reputation as a story writer was firmly established by the publication in national magazines of more than a dozen successful tales later gathered in The Long Valley. In the 1940s and 50s, Steinbeck continued to experiment with the short story form both as a fiction writer and a journalist. While some bolder experiments of these last decades fall short of his earlier efforts, others can be counted among his best stories.

During the span of his career, Steinbeck won the O. Henry Memorial Award four times--in 1934 ("The Murder"), 1938 ("The Promise"), 1942 ("How Edith McGillcuddy Met R.L. Stevenson"), and 1956 ("Affair at 7, Rue de M---"). In addition, several other Steinbeck tales have been honored by inclusion in prestigious and selective anthologies: "The

Chrysanthemums" in 50 Best American Stories 1915-1965
(1966), "The Snake" in Great American Short Stories (1966),
"The Harness" in 50 Great American Stories (1966), "Flight"
in Short Story Masterpieces (1954), and the list could go
on.[39] These awards and honors indicate that Steinbeck
wrote some of the most highly acclaimed short fiction of his
era.   Certainly The Red Pony has earned an enduring place
in American literature, and "The Chrysanthemums," "Flight"
and perhaps even the later "How Mr. Hogan Robbed a Bank"
deserve the ultimate praise "Masterpiece."

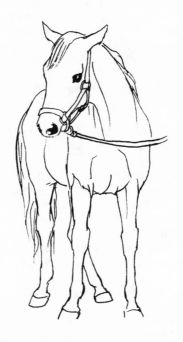

CHAPTER NOTES

CHAPTER ONE

1. Arthur Mizener, "Does a Moral Vision of the Thirties Deserve a Nobel Prize?" New York Times Book Review,
Dec. 9, 1962, pp. 4, 43-45.
2. Ray B. West, Jr., The Short Story in America,
1900-1950, (Freeport, N.Y.: Books for Libraries Press,
1968), pp. 45-51; Arthur Voss, The American Short Story:
A Critical Survey, (Norman: University of Oklahoma Press,
1973), pp. 268-73.
3. Frank Magill, Ed. Critical Survey of Short Fiction,
(Englewood Cliffs, N.J.: Salem Press, 1981), pp. 2274-2279.
4. See Peter Lisca, The Wide World of John Steinbeck
(New Brunswick, N.J.: Rutgers University Press, 1958),
and Warren French, John Steinbeck, 2nd rev. ed. (Boston:
Twayne Publishers, 1975).
5. Robert J. DeMott, Steinbeck's Reading: A Catalogue of Books Owned and Borrowed, (New York: Garland
Publishing, 1984), p. xxiii.
6. John Steinbeck, "Preface to the Compass Edition"
in Story Writing by Edith Roland Mirrielees (New York:
Viking Press, 1962).
7. DeMott, p. xxiv.
8. Anthoni Gajewski, "Nowelistyka Johna Steinbecka w
latach miedzwojennych," Diss. Institute of English Philology
at Adam Michiewicz University, Poznan, Poland 1970, pp.
105-125.
9. See Mizener, "Does a Moral Vision of the Thirties
Deserve a Nobel Prize?"
10. Gajewski, p. 121.
11. Thomas Kiernan. The Intricate Music: A Biography of John Steinbeck (Boston: Little, Brown, 1979) pp.
61, 64, 72.
12. Nelson Valjean, John Steinbeck, The Errant Knight:

An Intimate Biography of His California Years, (San Francisco: Chronicle Books, 1975), p. 58.

13. Lisca, p. 24.

14. Joseph Fontenrose, _John Steinbeck: An Introduction and Interpretation_ (New York: Barnes and Noble, 1963), p. 19.

15. Kiernan, p. 89.

16. Valjean, pp. 73-4.

17. John Steinbeck, "Fingers of Cloud: A Satire on College Protervity," in _Stanford Writers, 1891-1941_, ed. Violet L. Shue, (Stanford University: Dramatists' Alliance, 1941), p. 104. All further references to this work appear in the text.

18. John Steinbeck, _Of Mice and Men_ (New York: Covici-Friede, 1937), pp. 34-35.

19. John Steinbeck, "Adventures in Arcademy: A Journey into the Ridiculous," _Stanford Spectator_, 2 (June 1924), 279. All further references to this work appear in the text.

20. Valjean, p. 74.

21. Letter received from Carlton A. Sheffield, 27 February 1980.

22. Kiernan, p. 90. Also see Edith Roland Mirrielees, _Writing the Short Story_ (New York: Doubleday, 1929), p. 104.

23. Sheffield, letter 27 Feb. 1980.

24. Jackson J. Benson, _The True Adventures of John Steinbeck, Writer_, (New York: Viking, 1984), pp. 88-89.

25. John Steinbeck, "Autobiography: Making of a New Yorker," _New York Times Magazine_, Feb. 1, 1953, p. 26.

26. Kiernan, p. 107.

27. Steinbeck, "Autobiography: Making of a New Yorker," p. 27.

28. Kiernan, p. 114.

29. Valjean, pp. 100-101.

30. Letter received from Carlton A. Sheffield, 8 March 1980.

31. Letter received from Amasa Miller, 22 March 1980.

32. Benson, pp. 76-77.

33. Carlton A. Sheffield, Intro, _Letters to Elizabeth: A Selection of Letters from John Steinbeck to Elizabeth Otis_, eds. Florian J. Shasky and Susan F. Riggs (San Francisco, Calif.: The Book Club of California, 1978), p. xiv-xv.

34. Miller, letter 22 March 1980.

35. Benson, p. 77.

36. Clifford L. Lewis, "Four Dubious Steinbeck Stories," Steinbeck Quarterly, 5 (1972), pp. 17-19.

37. Miller, letter 22 March 1980.

38. "To Wilbur Needham," [Early 1935], Steinbeck: A Life in Letters, Elaine Steinbeck and Robert Wallsten, eds. (New York: Viking, 1975), p. 106.

39. Kiernan, p. 193.

40. Letter received from Lawrence Clark Powell, 16 February 1980.

41. See Robert S. Hughes, Jr. "Steinbeck Stories at the Houghton Library: A Case for Authenticity of Four Unpublished Texts," Harvard Library Bulletin XXX (Jan. 1982), pp. 87-95.

42. Valjean, p. 98.

43. Miller, letter 22 March 1980.

44. Walter F. Taylor, The Economic Novel in America (Chapel Hill, N.C.: The University of North Carolina Press, 1942), pp. 80-82.

45. John Steinbeck (attributed author), "East Third Street," TS. The Houghton Library, AL 3523.20.21.

46. John Steinbeck [Untitled Christmas Story] TS. The Steinbeck Collection, Department of Special Collections, Stanford University Libraries.

47. To Margaret Gemmell, ca. 1926, The Steinbeck Collection, Department of Special Collections, Stanford University Libraries.

48. Dook Sheffield to Margaret Gemmell, ca. 1978 TS. The Steinbeck Collection, Department of Special Collections, Stanford University Libraries.

49. Dook Sheffield to Margaret Gemmell, ca. 1978.

50. DeMott, (p. 24) lists among Steinbeck's reading: "The Autobiography of Benvenuto Cellini. Trans. by J.A. Symonds. New York: Collier, 1910."

51. Benson, pp. 92-93.

52. John Steinbeck, "The White Sister of Fourteenth Street," TS. The Steinbeck Collection, Department of Special Collections, Stanford University Libraries.

53. The Oxford Companion to Film, ed. Liz-Anne Bawden (London: Oxford University Press, 1976), p. 291.

54. The American Film Institute Catalogue of Motion Pictures Produced in the United States (New York: R.R. Bowker Co., 1971), pp. 895-6.

55. John Pilkington, Francis Marion Crawford, Twayne United States Authors Series, No. 67 (New York: Twayne Publishers, 1964), p. 183.

56. Mollie B. Steinberg, The History of the Fourteenth Street Theatre (New York: Dial Press, 1931), p. 79. Also see "Clemente Gilio," obituary, New York Times, 16 July 1943.
57. Benson, p. 97.
58. John Steinbeck (attributed author), "The Nymph and Isobel," TS. The Houghton Library, AL 3523.20.62.
59. Benson, p. 75.
60. Jacob A. Riis, How the Other Half Lives (New York: Charles Scribner's Sons, 1890), p. 234.
61. John Steinbeck (attributed author), "The Days of Long Marsh," TS. The Houghton Library, AL 3523.20.16.
62. Lawrence W. Jones, "A Note on Steinbeck's Earliest Stories," Steinbeck Quarterly, 2 (Fall 1969), p. 60.
63. Miller, letter 22 March 1980.
64. John Steinbeck (attributed author), "The Nail" TS. The Houghton Library, AL 3523.20.58. The Sisera and Jael story appears in Judges iv. 17-22 and v. 24-27.
65. Benson, p. 75. If Benson is correct, "The Nail" must have been written later than the 1924-26 dates I have estimated.
66. Benson, p. 77.
67. Jones, pp. 59-60.
68. Valjean, p. 107.
69. John Steinbeck (Pseud. John Stern), "The Gifts of Iban," The Smokers Companion, 1 (March 1927), 18. All further references to this work appear in the text.
70. Fontenrose, p. 9.
71. Kiernan. p. 113.
72. Kiernan, p. 114; 118-119.

CHAPTER TWO

1. Richard Astro, John Steinbeck and Edward F. Ricketts: The Shaping of a Novelist (Minneapolis, Minn.: University of Minnesota Press, 1973), p. 96.
2. "To Mavis McIntosh," 8 May 1931, Steinbeck: A Life in Letters, p. 43.
3. Joseph Fontenrose, Steinbeck's Unhappy Valley (Berkeley, Calif.: Albany Press, 1981), pp. 9; 15.
4. New York Evening Post, Saturday, 29 Oct. 1932, p. 7.
5. Harry Thornton Moore, The Novels of John Steinbeck: A First Critical Study, 2nd ed. (Port Washington, N.J.: Kennikat Press, 1968), p. 18.

6. French, 1975, p. 55.
7. "To Mavis McIntosh," 8 May 1931, Steinbeck: A
Life in Letters, p. 43.
8. John Steinbeck, The Pastures of Heaven (New
York: Brewer, Warren and Putnam, 1932), p. 27. All
further references to this work appear in the text.
9. See Mimi Reisel Gladstein, "Female Characters in
Steinbeck: Minor Characters of Major Importance?" in Steinbeck's Women: Essays in Criticism, Steinbeck Monograph
Series, No. 9, ed. Tetsumaro Hayashi (Muncie, Indiana:
Ball State University, 1979), pp. 21-22.
10. "Steinbeck's Strong Women: Feminine Identity in
the Short Stories," in Steinbeck's Women: Essays in Criticism, p. 103-4.
11. Astro, pp. 103-4.
12. Howard Levant, The Novels of John Steinbeck: A
Critical Study (Columbia, Missouri: University of Missouri
Press, 1974), p. 49.
13. Lisca, p. 64.
14. Kiernan, p. 163-4.
15. Astro, p. 96.
16. Adrian H. Goldstone and John R. Payne, eds.,
John Steinbeck: A Bibliographical Catalogue of the Adrian
H. Goldstone Collection (Austin, Tx.: University of Texas,
1974), pp. 24-25.
17. The story contains several allusions, two of which
I have managed to track down: p. 87: "Valesquez' Cardinal":
painting by Spanish artist Diego Rodriguez de Silva y Velas-
quez, 1599-1660. Since Valesquez painted several portraits
of various cardinals (ecclesiastical officials) it is hard to determine the exact portrait Steinbeck had in mind. P. 88:
David Grayson (pseud.), Adventures in Contentment (1907):
A narrative by progressive thinker Ray Stannard Baker,
1870-1946, concerning the adventures of fictive farmer,
David Grayson. Baker during this period was influenced by
Thoreau, Emerson, and Whitman, but his favorite book was
Stevenson's Travels with a Donkey (1879), which is also a
favorite of Steinbeck's protagonist, Junius Maltby. See
DeMott, items 173 & 767.
18. Richard F. Peterson, "The Turning Point: The
Pastures of Heaven (1932)," in A Study Guide to Steinbeck:
A Handbook to His Major Works, ed. Tetsumaro Hayashi
(Metuchen, N.J.: Scarecrow Press, 1974), pp. 94, 96.
19. See Randall R. Mawer, "Takashi Kato, 'Good
American' The Central Episode in Steinbeck's The Pastures

of Heaven," Steinbeck Quarterly 13 (Winter-Spring, 1980),
pp. 23-31.
    20. Valjean, pp. 19-20.
    21. See Moore, p. 30; Astro, pp. 81-83; and Levant,
pp. 43-44, n. 31.
    22. Levant, p. 43.
    23. "Steinbeck's Happy Hookers," in Steinbeck's Wom-
en: Essays in Criticism, p. 41.
    24. Gladstein, p. 18.
    25. Levant, p. 44.
    26. Peterson, p. 100.
    27. Fontenrose, p. 25; see also DeMott, items 386,
799, & 928.
    28. Astro, p. 103.

CHAPTER THREE

    1. Kiernan, p. 172.
    2. Fontenrose, p. 66.
    3. Eda Lou Walton, "The Simple Life," rev. of The
Long Valley, Nation 147 (Oct. 1, 1938), 331-332.
    4. Lewis Owens, John Steinbeck's Re-vision of America
(Athens, Georgia: University of Georgia Press), pp. 106-7.
    5. John Steinbeck, The Long Valley (New York: Vik-
ing Press, 1938), pp. 45, 171. All further references to this
work appear in the text.
    6. Owens, p. 107.
    7. Lisca, p. 93.
    8. Kiernan, pp. 225-26.
    9. Letters to Elizabeth, p. 6.
    10. Kiernan, p. 231.
    11. Lisca, p. 100.
    12. Brian Barbour, "Steinbeck as a Short Story
Writer," in A Study Guide to Steinbeck's "The Long Valley,"
ed. Tetsumaro Hayashi (Ann Arbor, Michigan: Pierian Press,
1976), p. 116.
    13. Edmund Wilson, Classics and Commercials: A Lit-
erary Chronicle of The Forties. (New York: Farrar, Straus,
and Co., 1950), pp. 36-37.
    14. Stanley Young, "The Short Stories of John Stein-
beck," rev. of The Long Valley, New York Times Book Review, 25 Sept. 1938, p. 7.
    15. Joseph Warren Beach, "John Steinbeck: Journey-
man Artist," in Steinbeck and His Critics: A Record of

Twenty-five Years, eds. E.W. Tedlock and C.V. Wicker
(Albuquerque, N.M.: University of New Mexico Press,
1957), p. 83.
    16. See Hayashi, Steinbeck's Women: Essays in Criti-
cism.
    17. Barbour, p. 122.
    18. Elmer Davis, "The Steinbeck Country," rev. of
The Long Valley, Saturday Review, 18 (Sept. 24, 1938), 11.
    19. Roy S. Simmonds, "The Original Manuscripts of
'The Chrysanthemums,'" Steinbeck Quarterly 7 (Summer-
Fall, 1974), 102-111.
    20. Actually, two variations on the finished text exist;
see William R. Osborn, "The Texts of Steinbeck's 'The Chrysanthemums,'" Modern Fiction Studies 12 (1966), 479-484.
    21. Simmonds, p. 106.
    22. Mitchell, pp. 27, 33.
    23. Barbour, p. 122.
    24. Simmonds, p. 106.
    25. Steinbeck: A Life in Letters, p. 91.
    26. Mitchell, p. 31.
    27. Steinbeck alludes to these matters on various pages
of the manuscript copybook owned by San Jose State University; see note "a" in the Chapter Four introduction.
    28. Kiernan, p. 195.
    29. The plot and characters in "The White Quail" are
startingly similar to those in Cannery Row chapter 24, which
contains a brief episode in the lives of Tom and Mary Talbot;
see the discussion of this tale in Chapter Four.
    30. Young, p. 7.
    31. Barbour, pp. 117-118.
    32. Arthur L. Simpson, "'The White Quail': A Portrait
of an Artist," in A Study Guide to Steinbeck's "The Long Valley," pp. 11-16.
    33. Astro, p. 116; Fontenrose, p. 62; French, 1975,
pp. 81-95; Lisca, p. 95. Also see Stanley Renner, "Sexual
Idealism and Violence in 'The White Quail'" Steinbeck Quarterly XVII (Summer-Fall), 1984, pp. 76-87.
    34. Gajewski, p. 75.
    35. John M. Ditsky, "Steinbeck's 'Flight': The Am-
biguity of Manhood," in A Study Guide to Steinbeck's "The
Long Valley," pp. 11-16.
    36. Twentieth-Century Short Story Explication: Inter-
pretations 1900-1975 of Short Fiction Since 1800, 3rd ed.
Warren S. Walker (Hamden, Conn.: Shoe String Press, 1977),
pp. 698-702.

37. New Republic, 103 (Dec. 9, 1940), 784-7.
38. Lisca, pp. 99-100. William M. Jones, in "Steinbeck's 'Flight,'" Explicator 18 (Nov. 1959) item 11, was the first critic after Lisca to offer an allegorical reading; Dan Vogel, in "Steinbeck's 'Flight: The Myth of Manhood," College English, 23 (1961), 225-26, also echoing Lisca's allegorical reading, says that Pepé is an Everyman and his flight becomes the universal journey toward attainment of manhood; Frederick Madeo, in " 'Flight'--An Allegorical Journey" English Record, 14 (1964), 55, claims to have discovered the influence of the Bible, specifically the stories of Adam and Eve and the Passion; John Antico, in "A Reading of Steinbeck's 'Flight,'" Modern Fiction Studies 11 (1965), 45-53, stresses that Pepé rises above primeval darkness to become a man. This view is shared by M.R. Satyanarayana in "And Then the Child Becomes A Man: Three Initiation Stories of John Steinbeck," Indian Journal of American Studies 1 (1971), 87-92. Later studies by Richard Astro, Robert M. Benton, and John M. Ditsky follow a similar line of reasoning. Thus Lisca's contention that "Flight" is a moral allegory which describes Pepé's initiation into manhood seems to have influenced subsequent interpretations.
39. Satyanarayana, p. 87.
40. See French, 1961, p. 142 and French, 1975, p. 68. Other critics like French have suggested that the story's meaning is discoverable on the literal level alone: Chester F. Chapin, in "Pepé Torres: A Steinbeck 'Natural,'" College English 23 (1962), 676, carries one aspect of French's argument to an extreme, by calling Pepé a "boy of subnormal intelligence." Similarly, Walter K. Gordon, in "Steinbeck's 'Flight': Journey to or from Maturity?" Studies in Short Fiction 3 (1966), 453-455, sees in "Flight" a pessimistic tale ending in tragedy. Likewise, Hilton Anderson, in "Steinbeck's 'Flight,'" The Explicator 28 (Oct. 1969) Item 12, chronicles Pepé's regression, but blames his death on a snake. While each of these interpretations varies somewhat from Wilson's 1940 reading, all share its basic tenet--that "Flight" is the Naturalistic tale of an immature youth's slow, but inevitable crawl to death.
41. Barbour, p. 64.
42. Antico, p. 51.
43. Chapin, p. 676.
44. Norman Friedman, "What Makes a Short Story Short?" Modern Fiction Studies 4 (1958), p. 113.
45. Owens, p. 34.

46. Gajewski, p. 67.
47. Lisca, p. 98.
48. John Steinbeck, "About Ed Ricketts," Intro. to
The Log From the Sea of Cortez (New York: Viking Press,
1951), pp. xxxiii-xxxiv.
49. A. Grove Day, March 4, 1985 lecture, University
of Hawaii at Manoa.
50. Charles E. May, "Myth and Mystery in Steinbeck's
'The Snake': A Jungian View," Criticism 15 (1973), p. 328.
51. "About Ed Ricketts," pp. xi-xxxix.
52. French, 1961, p. 82.
53. French, 1961, p. 82.
54. May, p. 330.
55. Lisca, p. 96.
56. Fontenrose, p. 63.
57. John Steinbeck, Sweet Thursday (New York:
Viking Press, 1954), p. 107.
58. C. Hugh Holman, A Handbook to Literature 3rd
ed. (New York: Bobbs-Merrill, 1972), p. 500.
59. For an opposing view, see Robert M. Benton,
"'Breakfast' I and II," in A Study Guide to Steinbeck's "The
Long Valley," p. 33.
60. See James A. Hamby, "Steinbeck's Biblical Vision:
'Breakfast' and the Nobel Prize Acceptance Speech," Western
Review 10 (Spring, 1973), 58; and Edwin M. Moseley, Pseudo-
nyms of Christ in the Modern Novel (Pittsburgh, Penn.: University of Pittsburgh Press, 1962), p. 182.
61. Benton, pp. 36-38, argues to the contrary.
62. Gajewski, p. 39.
63. Peter Lisca, "'The Raid' and In Dubious Battle,"
in A Study Guide to Steinbeck's "The Long Valley," p. 43.
64. Gajewski, p. 39.
65. Satyanarayana, pp. 87-88.
66. See Roy S. Simmonds, "The Original Manuscript
of 'The Chrysanthemums,'" p. 105.
67. At present a visit to the owner of the manuscript,
the Steinbeck Research Center in San Jose, California, is the
only way to read and study this valuable story. See note
"a" of Table I; Cox, pp. 96-99.
68. French, 1961, p. 83: Franklin E. Court, "A Vigilante's Fantasy," in A Study Guide to Steinbeck's "The Long
Valley," p. 55; Brian Barbour, pp. 114-5; and Gajewski,
p. 32.
69. Lisca, p. 97; Astro, p. 70.
70. Lisca, p. 96.

71. Valjean, p. 45.
72. Street, p. 40.
73. Wilson, Classics and Commercials, p. 42.
74. Lisca, p. 96.
75. See Warren French, "' Johnny Bear': Steinbeck's 'Yellow Peril' Story," in A Study Guide to Steinbeck's "The Long Valley," pp. 57-64.
76. "Steinbeck's 'The Murder' A Critical and Biographical Study," Steinbeck Quarterly 9 (Spring, 1976), 45.
77. Steve Crouch, Steinbeck Country (New York: Crown Publishers, 1973), p. 46.
78. "Steinbeck's 'The Murder,'" Studies in Short Fiction 14 (1977), 63.
79. Fontenrose, John Steinbeck, p. 60; Barbour, p. 119; French, 1961, p. 80.
80. "The Cryptic Raillery of 'Saint Katy the Virgin,'" in A Study Guide to Steinbeck's "The Long Valley," p. 73.
81. French, 1961, p. 87.
82. Wilson, Classics and Commercials, p. 37.
83. Marovitz, pp. 75-77.
84. Davis, p. 11.
85. John Steinbeck, "My Short Novels," in Steinbeck and His Critics, p. 38.
86. Kiernan. p. 175.
87. [1933] Steinbeck: A Life in Letters, p. 73.
88. "Steinbeck: Through a Glass, Though Brightly," Rev. of The Long Valley, New Republic 96 (Oct. 12, 1938), 274-5.
89. Mizener, p. 4.
90. Mizener, p. 4; Barbour, p. 122; French, 1975, p. 63.
91. French, 1975, p. 62.
92. Robert M. Benton, "Realism, Growth, and Contrast in 'The Gift,'" in A Study Guide to Steinbeck's "The Long Valley," p. 86.
93. French, 1961, p. 90.
94. Howard Levant, "John Steinbeck's The Red Pony: A Study in Narrative Technique," Journal of Narrative Technique, I (May, 1971), pp. 77-85.
95. Arnold L. Goldsmith, "Thematic Rhythm in The Red Pony," College English, 26 (1965), pp. 391-94.
96. Fontenrose, John Steinbeck, p. 64.
97. Levant, "Steinbeck's The Red Pony," p. 80.
98. Owens, p. 51.
99. Owens, pp. 11, 34.

100. French, 1961, p. 90.

101. Richard F. Peterson, "The Grail Legend and Stein-beck's 'The Great Mountains,'" Steinbeck Quarterly 6 (Winter 1973), p. 9.

102. Robert H. Woodward, "The Promise of Steinbeck's 'The Promise,'" in A Study Guide to Steinbeck's "The Long Valley," p. 98.

103. Levant, "Steinbeck's The Red Pony," p. 84.

104. Fontenrose, John Steinbeck, p. 64.

105. Wilfred L. Guerin, et al., A Handbook of Critical Approaches to Literature (New York: Harper and Row, 1966), p. 119.

106. The term "phalanx" is also discussed in the above section on "The Vigilante."

107. "'Westering' in 'The Leader of the People,'" Western American Literature 4 (Summer, 1969), 122-4.

108. "In Defense of 'Westering,'" Western American Literature 5 (Summer, 1970), 146.

109. "Steinbeck's 'The Leader of the People': A Crisis in Style," Western American Literature 5 (Summer, 1970), 138.

110. Barbour, pp. 125-26.

111. Mary Ellen Caldwell, "A New Consideration of the Intercalary Chapters in The Grapes of Wrath," Markham Review 3 (1971-72), p. 115.

112. Caldwell, p. 116.

113. Lisca, p. 157.

114. For a listing of these and similar excerpts from The Grapes of Wrath see Tetsumaro Hayashi, A New Stein-beck Bibliography, 1929-1971 (Metuchen, N.J.: Scarecrow Press, 1973), pp. 32-33.

115. See Hayashi, A New Steinbeck Bibliography, 1929-1971, pp. 31-37, which lists other fictional excerpts from Cannery Row, East of Eden, In Dubious Battle, The Moon is Down, Of Mice and Men, The Pastures of Heaven, Sweet Thursday, and The Winter of Our Discontent. Tor-tilla Flat has also been excerpted as short fiction in The Portable Steinbeck (New York: Viking Press, 1971 [1943, 1946 eds]).

CHAPTER FOUR

1. Portions of this chapter were originally published in the Steinbeck Quarterly XVIII (Summer-Fall, 1985), pp. 79-93.

2. On page one of a manuscript copybook owned by the Steinbeck Research Center at San Jose State University, Steinbeck lists "Edith McGillcuddy" among a group of "stories completed summer of 1934." Since Mrs. Edith Wagner initially expressed interest in publishing her own version of the story, Steinbeck withdrew his manuscript from his literary agents and did not attempt to publish it until several years later-- with Mrs. Wagner's blessing. See Robert H. Woodward, "John Steinbeck, Edith McGillcuddy, and Tortilla Flat," San Jose Studies 3 (1977), 70-73; and Robert S. Hughes, Jr., "Steinbeck's Short Stories: A Critical Study," Diss. Indiana University, 1981, pp. 175; 290-91.

3. John Steinbeck, "How Edith McGillcuddy Met R.L.S.," in The Portable Steinbeck rev. and enl. ed., ed. Lewis Gannet (New York: Viking Press, 1943), p. 572. All further references to this work appear in the text. The story was originally published in Harper's Magazine, 183 (Aug, 1941), 252-258.

4. See Roy S. Simmonds, "John Steinbeck, R.L. Stevenson, and Edith McGillcuddy," San Jose Studies, 1 (Nov, 1975), pp. 29-39.

5. Simmonds, p. 29.

6. John Steinbeck, Once There Was a War (New York: Viking Press, 1958), pp. 112-116. All further references to this work appear in the text. See also Hayashi, A New Steinbeck Bibliography, 1929-1971, p. 15, for a listing of Steinbeck's 1943 war dispatches in The New York Herald Tribune.

7. French, 1975, p. 28; Lisca, p. 185.

8. Lisca, p. 185.

9. In Pause to Wonder, ed. Marjorie Fischer and Rolfe Humphries (New York: Julian Messner, 1944), pp. 401-403.

10. Valjean, pp. 2-83.

11. Peter Lisca, The Wide World of John Steinbeck (New Brunswick, N.J.: Rutgers University Press, 1958), p. 212; see also Hughes, "Steinbeck's Short Stories," pp. 310-316.

12. "The Time the Wolves Ate the Vice-Principal," '47, Magazine of the Year, Vol. 1, No. 1 (March, 1947), 26-27. All further references to this work appear in the text.

13. French, pp. 110-20.

14. Lisca, p. 208.

15. Letters to Elizabeth, p. 14.

16. Lisca, pp. 211-212.

17. French, 1975, p. 117.

18. "The Miracle of Tepayac," Collier's, 122 (Dec. 25, 1948), p. 23.

19. See Donald Demarest and Coley Talor, eds., The Dark Virgin: The Book of Our Lady of Guadalupe, New York: Academy Guild Press, 1956.

20. "To Bo Beskow," 19 Nov. 1948 and 9 May 1949, Steinbeck: A Life in Letters, Elaine Steinbeck and Robert Wallsten, eds. (New York: Viking, 1975), pp. 341, 352.

21. Reader's Digest 55 (Sept. 1949), 19-21. All further references to this work appear in the text.

22. John Steinbeck, Sweet Thursday (New York: Viking Press, 1954), pp. 55-56. All further references to this work appear in the text.

23. "To Elizabeth Otis," 17 Sept. 1954, Steinbeck: A Life in Letters, p. 497.

24. "To Mr. and Mrs. Elia Kazan," 14 Sept. 1954, Steinbeck: A Life in Letters, p. 496.

25. John Steinbeck, "The Affair at 7, Rue de M---," Harper's Bazaar No. 1, 2921 (April, 1955), 112, 202, 213; reprinted in Prize Stories 1956: The O. Henry Awards, eds. Paul Engle and Hansford Martin (New York: Double-day, 1956), p. 262. All further references to this work appear in the text.

26. "The Summer Before," Punch, 128 (May 25, 1955), p. 649. All further references to this work appear in the text.

27. Original title: "We're Holding Our Own," Lilliput, 37 (Nov. 1955), 18-19; appeared later as "The Short-Short Story of Mankind" in Playboy 5 (April, 1958). The text cited here is from The Permanent Playboy, ed. Ray Russell (New York: Crown Publishers, 1959), 325-29.

28. Lawrence William Jones, "An Uncited Post-War Steinbeck Story: 'The Short Short Story of Mankind,'" Steinbeck Quarterly, 3 (1970), 30-31.

29. Warren French, "Steinbeck's Winter Tale," Modern Fiction Studies 11 (1965), 66; French also explains the rela-tionship between the story, "Mr. Hogan," and the novel Steinbeck generated from it, The Winter of Our Discontent (1961).

30. "How Mr. Hogan Robbed a Bank," Atlantic Month-ly, 197 (March, 1956), 58-61, p. 61. All further references to this work appear in the text.

31. Warren French, John Steinbeck. Twayne United States Authors Series, No. 2 (New York: Twayne Publishers, 1961), p. 170.

32. "To Elizabeth Otis," 7 March 1956, Letters to Elizabeth, p. 65.

33. French, "Steinbeck's Winter Tale," p. 68.
34. French, John Steinbeck, 1975, p. 160.
35. French, John Steinbeck, 1961, p. 170.
36. Kiernan, pp. 299, 304, 310.
37. "Reunion at the Quiet Hotel," [London] Evening Standard, Jan. 25, 1958, p. 9. All further references to this work appear in the text. Roy S. Simmonds kindly acquainted me with the earlier Courier-Journal text.
38. Kiernan, p. 310.
39. See Tetsumaro Hayashi, A New Steinbeck Bibliography, 1971-1981 (Metuchen, N.J.: Scarecrow Press, 1983), pp. 7-14.

SELECTED BIBLIOGRAPHY

PRIMARY SOURCES

I. Published Stories
(chronological by date of first publication)

"Fingers of Cloud: A Satire on College Protervity," Stanford Spectator, 2 (Feb. 1924), 149, 161-164.

"Adventures in Arcademy: A Journey Into the Ridiculous," Stanford Spectator, 2 (June 1924), 279, 291.

"The Gifts of Iban," (by John Stern, pseud.), The Smokers Companion, 1 (March 1927), 18-19, 70-72.

"The Red Pony," (appeared in The Long Valley as "The Gift"), North American Review, 236 (Nov., 1933), 421-38.

"The Great Mountains," North American Review, 236 (Dec., 1933), 492-500.

"The Murder," North American Review, 237 (April, 1934), 305-312.

"The Raid," North American Review, 238 (Oct., 1934), 299-305.

"The White Quail," North American Review, 239 (March, 1935), 204-211.

"The Snake," Monterey Beacon, I (June 22, 1935), 10-11. 14-15.

"The Leader of the People," Argosy [London], 20 (Aug., 1936), 99-106.

"The Lonesome Vigilante," Esquire, 6 (Oct., 1936), 35,
    186A-186B. (Appeared in The Long Valley as "The
    Vigilante").

"Breakfast," Pacific Weekly, 5 (Nov. 9, 1936), 300.

"Saint Katy the Virgin," Covici-Friede monograph, Christmas,
    1936.

"The Promise," Harper's Magazine, 175 (Aug., 1937), 243-
    252.

"The Ears of Johnny Bear," Esquire, 8 (Sept., 1937), 35,
    195-200. (Appeared in The Long Valley as "Johnny
    Bear").

"The Chrysanthemums," Harper's Magazine, 175 (Oct., 1937),
    513-519.

"The Harness," Atlantic Monthly, 161 (June, 1938), 741-749.

"Flight," first published in The Long Valley, Viking Press,
    1938.

"How Edith McGillcuddy Met R.L. Stevenson," Harper's
    Magazine, 183 (Aug., 1941), 252-258.

"The Time the Wolves Ate the Vice Principal," rejected inter-
    chapter from Cannery Row, '47, The Magazine of the Year,
    vol. 1, no. 1 (March, 1947), 26-27.

"Miracle of Tepayac," Collier's, 122 (Dec. 25, 1948), 22-23.

"His Father," Reader's Digest, 55 (Sept., 1949), 19-21.

"The Affair at 7, Rue de M---," Harper's Bazaar, No. 2921
    (April, 1955), 112, 202, 213.

"The Summer Before," Punch, 128 (May 25, 1955), 647-51.

"We're Holding Our Own," Lilliput, 37 (Nov., 1955), 18-19.
    (Appeared later in Playboy, 5 (April, 1958) as "The Short-
    Short Story of Mankind").

"How Mr. Hogan Robbed a Bank," Atlantic Monthly, 197
    (March, 1956), 58-61.

"Case of the Hotel Ghost--Or ... What Are You Smoking In
    That Pipe, Mr. S.?," Louisville Courier-Journal, June 30,
    1957, Section 4, p. 3. (Appeared later in the London
    Evening Standard, Jan. 25, 1958, p. 9, as "Reunion at
    the Quiet Hotel.")

II. Unpublished Stories
(by date of composition)

"The Days of Long Marsh," ca. 1926, TS. The Houghton
    Library, AL 3523.20.16.

"East Third Street," ca. 1926, TS, The Houghton Library,
    AL 3523.20.21.

"The Nail," ca. 1926, TS. The Houghton Library, AL
    3523.20.58.

"The Nymph and Isobel," ca. 1926, TS. The Houghton Li-
    brary, AL 3523.20.62.

"The White Sister of Fourteenth Street," ca. 1926, TS. The
    Steinbeck Collection, Department of Special Collections,
    Stanford University Libraries.

Untitled Christmas story, ca. 1926, TS. The Steinbeck Col-
    lection, Department of Special Collections, Stanford Uni-
    versity Libraries.

"Unnamed Narrative," ca. 1929, MS. The Steinbeck Collec-
    tion, Department of Special Collections, Stanford Univer-
    sity Libraries.

"Case History," ca. 1934, MS. Steinbeck Research Center,
    San Jose State University.

III. Books by Steinbeck Containing
Short Fiction

Cannery Row. New York: Viking Press, 1945.

The Grapes of Wrath. New York: Viking Press, 1939.

The Long Valley. New York: Viking Press, 1938.

Once There Was a War. New York: Viking Press, 1958.

The Pastures of Heaven. New York: Brewer, Warren, and
   Putnam 1932.

Sweet Thursday. New York: Viking Press, 1954.

Tortilla Flat. New York: Covici-Friede, 1935.

SECONDARY SOURCES

I. Bibliographies

Goldstone, Adrian H., and John R. Payne. John Steinbeck:
   A Bibliographical Catalogue of the Adrian H. Goldstone
   Collection. Austin: University of Texas, 1974.

Gross, John, and Lee Richard Hayman, eds. John Steinbeck: A Guide to the Collection of the Salinas Public
   Library. Salinas, Cal.: Salinas Public Library, 1979.

Hayashi, Tetsumaro, ed. John Steinbeck: A Concise Bibliography (1930-1965). Metuchen, N.J.: Scarecrow Press,
   1967.

_____. John Steinbeck: A Guide to the Doctoral Disserta-
   tions (A Collection of Dissertation Abstracts, 1946-69).
   Muncie, Ind.: Ball State University, (Steinbeck Society:
   Steinbeck Monograph Series, No. 1), 1971.

_____. A New Steinbeck Bibliography, 1929-1971.
   Metuchen, N.J.: Scarecrow Press, 1973.

_____. Steinbeck Criticism: A Review of Book-Length
   Studies (1939-1973). Muncie, Ind.: John Steinbeck Society of America, Steinbeck Monograph Series, No. 4.
   1974.

_____. A New Steinbeck Bibliography, 1971-1981,
   Metuchen, N.J.: Scarecrow Press, 1983. (See pp. 35-39

for an extensive list of Steinbeck bibliographies and bibliographical essays.)

II. Biographies

Bennett, Robert. The Wrath of John Steinbeck. Los
Angeles: Albertson Press, 1939.

Benson, Jackson J. The True Adventures of John Steinbeck, Writer. New York: Viking Press, 1984.

Champney, Freeman. "John Steinbeck, Californian." Steinbeck: A Collection of Critical Essays, ed. Robert Murray
Davis. Englewood Cliffs, N.J.: Prentice-Hall, 1972.

Gannett, Lewis. "John Steinbeck's Way of Writing" and
"Biographical and Bibliographical Note." The Portable
Steinbeck. New York: Viking Press, 1957, pp. vii-xxx.

Jackson, Joseph Henry. "John Steinbeck, A Portrait."
Saturday Review of Literature, 16 (Sept. 25, 1937), 11-
12, 18.

Kiernan, Thomas, The Intricate Music: A Biography of John
Steinbeck. Boston: Little, Brown, 1979.

Lisca, Peter. "John Steinbeck: A Literary Biography."
Steinbeck and His Critics, ed. E.W. Tedlock, Jr. and
C.V. Wicker. Albuquerque: University of New Mexico
Press, 1957.

Moore, Harry Thornton. "A Biographical Sketch." The
Novels of John Steinbeck, A First Critical Study, 2nd ed.
Port Washington, N.Y.: Kennikat Press, 1968 (1939),
pp. 73-96.

Valjean, Nelson. John Steinbeck, An Intimate Biography of
His California Years. San Francisco: Chronicle Books,
1975.

(See Hayashi, Tetsumaro, A New Steinbeck Bibliography,
1971-1981, pp. 39-42, for an extensive list of biographical books and essays on Steinbeck.)

III. Criticism and Scholarship on Steinbeck

A. Books and Dissertations

Astro, Richard. John Steinbeck and Edward F. Ricketts,
     The Shaping of a Novelist. Minneapolis: University of
     Minnesota Press, 1973.

Crouch, Steve. Steinbeck Country. New York: Crown
     Publishers, 1973.

DeMott, Robert J. Steinbeck's Reading: A Catalogue of
     Books Owned and Borrowed. New York: Garland Pub-
     lishing, 1984.

Fontenrose, Joseph. John Steinbeck: An Introduction and
     Interpretation. New York: Barnes and Noble, 1963.

French, Warren. John Steinbeck. Twayne United States
     Authors Series, No. 2. New York: Twayne Publishers,
     1961.

French, Warren. John Steinbeck. Twayne United States
     Authors Series, No. 2, 2nd rev. ed. Boston: Twayne
     Publishers, 1975.

Gajewski, Antoni. "Nowelistyka Johna Steinbecka w latach
     miedzwojennych," Diss. Institute of English Philology at
     Adam Michiewicz University, Poznon, Poland, 1970.

Levant, Howard. The Novels of John Steinbeck: A Critical
     Study. Columbia: University of Missouri Press, 1974.

Lisca, Peter. John Steinbeck: Nature and Myth. New
     York: Thomas Y. Crowell, Co., 1978.

_____. The Wide World of John Steinbeck. New Bruns-
     wick, N.J.: Rutgers University Press, 1958.

Marks, Lester Jay. Thematic Design in the Novels of John
     Steinbeck. The Hague, Netherlands: Mouton, 1969.

Moore, Harry Thornton. The Novels of John Steinbeck: A
     First Critical Study, 2nd ed. Port Washington, N.Y.:
     Kennikat Press, 1968.

O'Connor, Richard. John Steinbeck. New York: McGraw-
Hill, 1970.

Owens, Lewis. Steinbeck's Re-Vision of America. Athens:
University of Georgia Press, 1985.

Pratt, John Clark. John Steinbeck, Contemporary Writers
in Christian Perspective series. Grand Rapids, Mich.:
William B. Eerdmans, 1970.

Watt, F.W. Steinbeck. Edinburgh: Oliver and Boyd, 1962.

          B. Articles, Collections, and Parts of Books

Anderson, Hilton. "Steinbeck's 'Flight.'" Explicator, 28
(Oct. 1969), Item. 12.

Antico, John. "A Reading of Steinbeck's 'Flight.'" Modern
Fiction Studies, 11 (1965), 45-53.

Barbour, Brian. "Steinbeck as a Short Story Writer." In
A Study Guide to Steinbeck's "The Long Valley." Ed.
Tetsumaro Hayashi. Ann Arbor, Mich.: Pierian Press,
1976, pp. 113-128.

Beach, Joseph Warren. American Fiction, 1920-1940. New
York: MacMillan, 1941, pp. 309-347.

Benton, Robert M. "Breakfast." In A Study Guide to Steinbeck's "The Long Valley." Ed. Tetsumaro Hayashi. Ann
Arbor, Mich.: Pierian Press, 1976, pp. 33-40.

_____. "Realism, Growth, and Contrast in 'The Gift.'"
In A Study Guide to Steinbeck's "The Long Valley." Ed.
Tetsumaro Hayashi. Ann Arbor, Mich.: Pierian Press,
1976, pp. 81-88.

_____. "Steinbeck's The Long Valley (1938)." In A Study
Guide to Steinbeck: A Handbook to his Major Works. Ed.
Tetsumaro Hayashi. Metuchen, N.J.: Scarecrow Press,
1974, pp. 69-86.

Caldwell, Mary Ellen. "A New Consideration of the Intercalary Chapters in The Grapes of Wrath." Markham Review,
3 (1971-72), 115.

Chapin, Chester, F. "Pepé Torres: A Steinbeck 'Natural.'"
College English, 23 (1962), 676.

Cox, Martha Heasley. "The Steinbeck Collection in the Steinbeck Research Center, San Jose State University." Steinbeck Quarterly, 11 (1978), 96-99.

Davis, Elmer. "The Steinbeck Country." Review of The
Long Valley, by John Steinbeck. Saturday Review, 18
(Sept. 24, 1938), 11.

Davis, Robert Murray, ed. Steinbeck: A Collection of Critical Essays. Englewood Cliffs, N.J.: Prentice-Hall, 1972.

_____. "Steinbeck's 'The Murder.'" Studies in Short
Fiction, 14 (1977), 63-68.

Ditsky, John. "Steinbeck's 'Flight': The Ambiguity of Manhood." In A Study Guide to Steinbeck's "The Long Valley." Ed. Tetsumaro Hayashi. Ann Arbor, Mich.:
Pierian Press, 1976, pp. 17-24.

Fadiman, Clifton. Review of The Long Valley, by John
Steinbeck. New Yorker, 14 (Sept. 24, 1938), 72.

Friedman, Norman. "What Makes a Short Story Short?"
Modern Fiction Studies, 4 (1958), 103-117.

French, Warren. "'Johnny Bear': Steinbeck's 'Yellow Peril'
Story." In A Study Guide to Steinbeck's "The Long Val-
ley." Ed. Tetsumaro Hayashi. Ann Arbor, Mich.:
Pierian Press, 1976, pp. 57-64.

_____. "Steinbeck's Winter Tale." Modern Fiction Studies,
11 (1965), 66-74.

Galdstein, Mimi Reisel. "Female Characters in Steinbeck:
Minor Characters of Major Importance?" In Steinbeck's
Women: Essays in Criticism, Muncie, Ind.: Ball State
University, 1979, Steinbeck Monograph Series, No. 9.
Ed. Tetsumaro Hayashi. pp. 17-25.

Goldsmith, Arnold L. "Thematic Rhythm in The Red Pony."
College English, 26 (1965), 391-4.

150   Beyond The Red Pony

Gordon, Walter K. "Steinbeck's 'Flight': Journey to or from
Maturity?" Studies in Short Fiction, 3 (1966), 453-55.

Hamby, James A. "Steinbeck's Biblical Vision: 'Breakfast'
and the Nobel Prize Acceptance Speech." Western Review,
10 (Spring, 1973), 57-59.

Hayashi, Tetsumaro, ed. A Study Guide to Steinbeck's "The
Long Valley." Ann Arbor, Mich.: Pierian Press, 1976.

_____. A Study Guide to Steinbeck: A Handbook to his
Major Works. Metuchen, N.J.: Scarecrow Press, 1974.

Houghton, Donald. "'Westering' in 'The Leader of the People." Western American Literature, 4 (Summer, 1969),
117-124.

Jones, Lawrence W. "A Note on Steinbeck's Earliest Stories."
Steinbeck Quarterly, 2 (Fall, 1969), 59-60.

_____. "An Uncited Post-War Steinbeck Story: 'The Short
Short Story of Mankind.'" Steinbeck Quarterly, 3 (1970),
30-31.

Jones, William M. "Steinbeck's 'Flight.'" Explicator, 18
(Nov. 1959), Item 11.

Levant, Howard. "John Steinbeck's The Red Pony: A Study
in Narrative Technique." Journal of Narrative Technique,
I (May, 1971), 77-85.

Lewis, Clifford L. "Four Dubious Steinbeck Stories." Steinbeck Quarterly, 5 (1972), 17-19.

Lisca, Peter. "'The Raid' and In Dubious Battle." In A
Study Guide to Steinbeck's "The Long Valley." Ed.
Tetsumaro Hayashi. Ann Arbor, Mich.: Pierian Press,
1976, pp. 41-46.

Madeo, Frederick. "'Flight'--An Allegorical Journey."
English Record, 14 (1964), 55-58.

Marcus, Mordecai. "The Lost Dream of Sex and Childbirth."
Modern Fiction Studies, 11 (1965), 54-8.

Marovitz, Sanford. "The Cryptic Raillery of 'Saint Katy the
  Virgin.'" In A Study Guide to Steinbeck's "The Long
  Valley." Ed. Tetsumaro Hayashi. Ann Arbor, Mich.:
  Pierian Press, 1976, pp. 73-80.

Mawer, Randall R. "Takashi Kato, 'Good American': The
  Central Episode in Steinbeck's The Pastures of Heaven."
  Steinbeck Quarterly, 13 (Winter-Spring, 1980), 23-31.

May, Charles E. "Myth and Mystery in Steinbeck's 'The
  Snake'" A Jungian View." Criticism, 15 (1973), 322-35.

Miller, William V. "Sexual and Spiritual Ambiguity in 'The
  Chrysanthemums.'" In A Study Guide to Steinbeck's
  "The Long Valley." Ed. Tetsumaro Hayashi. Ann Arbor,
  Mich.: Pierian Press, 1976, pp. 1-10.

Mitchell, Marilyn L. "Steinbeck's Strong Women: Feminine
  Identity in the Short Stories." In Steinbeck's Women:
  Essays in Criticism, Muncie, Ind.: Ball State University,
  1979, Steinbeck Monograph Series, No. 9. Ed. Tetsumaro
  Hayashi. pp. 26-35.

Mizener, Arthur. "Does a Moral Vision of the Thirties Deserve a Nobel Prize?" New York Times Book Review,
  Dec. 9, 1962, pp. 4, 43-45.

Morsberger, Robert E. "In Defense of 'Westering.'" Western
  American Literature, 5 (Summer, 1970), 143-6.

_____. "Steinbeck's Happy Hookers." In Steinbeck's
  Women: Essays in Criticism, Muncie, Ind.: Ball State
  University, 1979, Steinbeck Monograph Series, No. 9.
  Ed. Tetsumaro Hayashi. pp. 36-48.

Osborn, William R. "The Texts of Steinbeck's 'The Chrysanthemums.'" Modern Fiction Studies, 12 (1966), 479-484.

Review of The Pastures of Heaven, by John Steinbeck.
  Booklist, 29 (Dec. 1, 1932), p. 116.

Review of The Pastures of Heaven, by John Steinbeck.
  New York Evening Post, Saturday, 29 Oct. 1932, p. 7.

Review of The Pastures of Heaven, by John Steinbeck.

    <u>Saturday Review of Literature</u>, 26 Nov. 1932, pp.
    275-6.

Peterson, Richard F. "The Turning Point: <u>The Pastures of</u>
    <u>Heaven</u> (1932)." In <u>A Study Guide to Steinbeck: A Hand-</u>
    <u>book to His Major Works</u>. Ed. Tetsumaro Hayashi.
    Metuchen, N.J.: Scarecrow Press, 1974, pp. 87-106.

_____. "The Grail Legend and Steinbeck's 'The Great
    Mountains.'" <u>Steinbeck Quarterly</u>, 6 (Winter, 1973),
    pp. 9-15.

Riggs, Susan F. "The Steinbeck Collection in the Depart-
    ment of Special Collections, Stanford University Librar-
    ies." <u>Steinbeck Quarterly</u>, 11 (1978), 102.

Satyanarayana, M.R. "And Then The Child Becomes a Man:
    Three Initiation Stories of John Steinbeck." <u>Indian Jour-</u>
    <u>nal of American Studies</u>, 1 (1971), 87-92.

Sheffield, Carlton A. Intro. to <u>Letters to Elizabeth: A</u>
    <u>Selection of Letters from John Steinbeck to Elizabeth Otis</u>.
    Eds. Florian J. Shasky and Susan F. Riggs. San Fran-
    cisco: The Book Club of California, 1978, pp. vii-xix.

Simmonds, Roy S. "The Original Manuscripts of "The Chry-
    santhemums.'" <u>Steinbeck Quarterly</u>, 7 (1974), 102-111.

_____. "John Steinbeck, R.L. Stevenson, and Edith
    McGillcuddy." <u>San Jose Studies</u>, 1 (Nov. 1975), 29-39.

_____. "Steinbeck's 'The Murder': A Critical and Bio-
    graphical Study." <u>Steinbeck Quarterly</u>, 9 (1976), 45.

Simpson, Arthur L. "'The White Quail': A Portrait of an
    Artist." In <u>A Study Guide to Steinbeck's "The Long</u>
    <u>Valley</u>." Ed. Tetsumaro Hayashi. Ann Arbor, Mich.:
    Pierian Press, 1976, pp. 11-16.

Street, Webster. "John Steinbeck: A Reminiscence." In
    <u>Steinbeck: The Man and His Work</u>. Eds. Richard Astro
    and Tetsumaro Hayashi. Corvallis: Oregon State Uni-
    versity Press, 1971, pp. 35-41.

Tedlock, E.W., Jr. and C.V. Wicker. <u>Steinbeck and His</u>

Critics: A Record of Twenty-Five Years. Albuquerque: University of New Mexico Press, 1957.

Vogel, Dan. "Steinbeck's 'Flight': The Myth of Manhood." College English, 23 (1961), 225-6.

Walton, Eda Lou. "The Simple Life." Review of The Long Valley. Nation 147 (1 Oct. 1938), 331-332.

West, Philip J. "Steinbeck's 'The Leader of the People': A Crisis in Style." Western American Literature, 5 (1970), 137-141.

Wilson, Edmund, "The Californians: Storm and Steinbeck." New Republic, 103 (Dec. 9, 1940), 184-7.

_____. Classics and Commercials: A Literary Chronicle of the Forties. New York: Farrar, Straus, and Co., 1950, pp. 35-45.

Whipple, T.K. "Steinbeck: Through a Glass, Though Brightly." Review of The Long Valley, by John Steinbeck. New Republic 96 (Oct. 12, 1938), 274-5.

Woodward, Robert H. "John Steinbeck, Edith McGillcuddy, and Tortilla Flat." San Jose Studies, 3 (1977), 70-73.

_____. "The Promise of Steinbeck's 'The Promise.'" In A Study Guide to Steinbeck's "The Long Valley." Ed. Tetsumaro Hayashi. Ann Arbor, Mich.: Pierian Press, 1976, pp. 97-104.

Young, Stanley. "The Short Stories of John Steinbeck." Review of The Long Valley, by John Steinbeck. New York Times Book Review, 25 Sept. 1938, p. 7.

IV. Theory and Criticism of the Short Story

Bates, H.E. The Modern Short Story. London: Thomas Nelson and Sons, 1949.

Forrest L. Ingram. Representative Short Story Cycles of the Twentieth Century. The Hague: Mouton Press, 1971.

Grabo, Carl H. The Art of the Short Story. New York:
Charles Scribner's Sons, 1913.

Magill, Frank, ed. Critical Survey of Short Fiction.
Englewood Cliffs, N.J.: Salem Press, 1981, pp. 2274-
2279.

Matthews, Brander. The Philosophy of the Short Story.
New York: Peter Smith, 1931.

May, Charles E. Short Story Theories. Athens, Ohio:
Ohio University Press, 1976.

O'Brien, Edward J. The Advance of the American Short
Story, rev. ed. New York: Dodd, Mead, and Co., 1931.

O'Connor, Frank. The Lonely Voice: A Study of the Short
Story. Cleveland, Ohio: World Publishing Co., 1963.

O'Faolain, Sean. The Short Story, London: Collins,
1948.

Mirrielees, Edith Roland. Story Writing (with a preface by
John Steinbeck). Boston: The Writer, Inc., 1972,
(1947).

_____. Writing the Short Story. New York: Doubleday,
1929.

Peden, William. The American Short Story: Front Line in
the National Defense of Literature. Boston: Houghton
Mifflin, 1964.

Reid, Ian. The Short Story. New York: Barnes & Noble,
1977.

Ross, Danforth. The American Short Story. Minneapolis:
University of Minnesota Press, 1961.

Thurston, Jarvis, et al. Short Fiction Criticism, A Check-
list of Interpretation Since 1925 of Stories and Novelettes
(American, British, Continental), 1800-1958. Denver,
Colo.: Alan Swallow, 1960.

Voss, Arthur. The American Short Story, A Critical Survey.
Norman: University of Oklahoma, 1973.

Walker, Warren S. Twentieth-Century Short Story Explica-
tion, Interpretations, 1900-1975 or Short Fiction Since
1800. 3rd ed. Hamden, Conn.: Shoe String Press,
1977.

West, Ray B., Jr. The Short Story in America 1900-1950.
Freeport, N.Y.: Books for Libraries Press, 1968.

NAME INDEX

157

TOPICAL INDEX

WORKS BY STEINBECK (titles of books are capitalized)

Short Fiction

Other Works by Steinbeck

TO A GOD UNKNOWN   12, 41, 43, 66, 89
TORTILLA FLAT   6, 54, 138n
TRAVELS WITH CHARLEY   15
WINTER OF OUR DISCONTENT   122, 138n

FORMAL QUALITIES OF STEINBECK'S SHORT FICTION